Gratitude

My Blessings, From Bizoton to Virginia

Suzette Civil-Noel

TEACH Services, Inc.
P U B L I S H I N G
www.TEACHServices.com • (800) 367-1844

Copyright © 2024 Suzette Civil-Noel

Copyright © 2024 TEACH Services, Inc.

ISBN-13: 978-1-4796-1665-7 (Paperback)

ISBN-13: 978-1-4796-1666-4 (ePub)

Library of Congress Control Number: 2024910532

TEACH Services, Inc.
P U B L I S H I N G
www.TEACHServices.com • (800) 367-1844

Table of Contents

Introduction 5

CHAPTER ONE : My Mother 7

CHAPTER TWO : My Father 10

CHAPTER THREE : My Siblings.. 12

CHAPTER FOUR : Catholic! Were We? 22

CHAPTER FIVE : Arrival in the United States 32

CHAPTER SIX : Prayer.. 38

CHAPTER SEVEN : Medgar Evers College.................................. 41

CHAPTER EIGHT : Love... 44

CHAPTER NINE : The Sabbath 52

CHAPTER TEN : The Next Few Years...................................... 56

CHAPTER ELEVEN : My Friend Nolcy 63

CHAPTER TWELVE : Virginia.. 69

Bibliography 77

Introduction

I am not sure how to start my story because so many tragic, supernatural, and exciting events happened during my journey from Bizoton to Virginia—many things that shaped me and made me the woman that I am today. They are occurrences both in my visible and invisible world that were simultaneously simple and complicated, joyful and painful, desirable and undesirable. Born in the middle of the 1970s in Haiti to a fifty-year-old father and an eighteen-year-old mother, living alongside half brothers and sisters, some of which were old enough to be my mother and father, I was loved, protected, and cared for in an unusual way. People often ask what my mother saw in my father. I could tell you that my dad was a handsome man, a giver, and a provider, but I think my mother needed a father more than a husband. I never knew how unusual my family was because I was happy, protected, loved, and content. My sisters are named Gertha and Myrlène, and my brothers are Francky (Fanfan), Pierre-Richard, Wilner (Nènè), and Nazaire (Ti Sonson), who is resting in the grave waiting for resurrection day. They were all there for me while I was growing up.

> *They are occurrences both in my visible and invisible world that were simultaneously simple and complicated, joyful and painful, desirable and undesirable.*

Port-au-Prince, the capital of Haiti, the country of my birth.

CHAPTER ONE

My Mother

Although my mother, Christiana, passed away when I was ten years old, I remember her smile as vivid as if it was yesterday. I always remember one of her common Haitian proverbs: "*Lè w gen pitit se bouche nen w bwè dlo santi*," which means when you have children, you should be able to hold your nose and drink the smelly water. It's referring to the idea that when you have children, you need to be able to take on certain things that life throws at you in order to protect them. She always made sure that my younger brother and I were fed, dressed, and protected. One thing that she always told me, even when I was pretty young, was to never let anyone touch my underwear or ask to see it. I am glad she did because when I was about four years old, I remember a man told me to show him what color my underwear was. As soon as he told me, I went and told my Aunt Janita, whom I was visiting at that time. She screamed at the man and told him to never come to her house again. Later in my life, I heard that he used to take advantage of little girls. I could have been molested if my mother did not tell me about the red flags of child molesters. Because she told me early, that saved me from being sexually abused by that sick man! Now that I have children on my own, I make sure that I tell them that this world is filled of mentally deranged people who seek to take advantage of children for their selfish desires.

According to Kristen A. Jenson, the author of the best-selling children's book, *Good Pictures Bad Pictures,* there are three big red flags that are important to know when it comes to sexual molestation. However, she says that kids need to learn body safety boundaries in order to be able to identify red flags. It is important for children to know at a very young age that there are parts of their body that are private, and that is why they are covered and not supposed to be shown to people other than their parents and doctors on very specific occasions such as bathing or a doctor's check-up.

Even when my mother was still alive, she was not around too much to take care of me or my younger brother. She couldn't because she was often sick. I never really understood her illnesses. No one ever explained to me why she had to suffer so much as a young woman! Why did she have to be taken away from me and my little brother so frequently? Why couldn't she smile anymore? Why couldn't she recognize us when we went to see her? Why couldn't her words make sense anymore? Why was I looking at my beautiful mother and not able to communicate with her? Where was she? Although she was physically there, she no longer talked like herself. Even her smile became unfamiliar to me. I don't know why she had to be taken so far away to Marigot to get treatment while all the good doctors were in Port-au-Prince, the capital of Haiti.

After she got better, she was told not to come back to Bizoton, which is where I grew up. They told her that was where her sickness originated. However, after my father left the country in 1985 to go to the United States for a better life, she came back. She was again repeating her famous proverb: "*Lè w gen pitit, se bouche nen w bwè dlo santi.*" I never knew that that "*dlo santi*" or "smelly water" would ruin her life. She never had the opportunity to enjoy much in life. Although I did not fully understand what happened, I was old enough to know that she did not die a natural death. She was often spoken about like she was someone else. I eventually came to realize that her body had been the house of evil spirits. She did not have the opportunity to give that beautiful temple of hers to Jesus.

Who else could have given her victory over the demons that were tormenting her? She did not know to just call on Jesus, who is the Lion of the tribe of Judah (see Rev. 5:5)! She did not know that all things are possible when we call on Jesus. She did not know that Jesus had died so that we can be free from the bondage of all evil spirits. She did not know that the Lord was her Shepherd; she shall not want. He could make her to lie down in green pastures; He could lead her beside the still waters and restore her soul (see Ps. 23). She did not claim the promises of God for her freedom. She did not know that all nations may have surrounded her, but in the name of the Lord, she could have destroyed them (see Ps. 118:10). She did not know to claim her victory by the blood of the Lamb that was slain on Calvary for the salvation of anyone who turned to Him.

One evening, one of the worst evenings of my life, I was on my bed ready to go to sleep when I heard her screaming like she was in exaggerated pain. I was old enough to feel her pain, to share her tears, but there was nothing I could do. I wish I had known about Jesus! I wish I had known what I know today! Oh Lord! I wish I had been able to do something that horrible night!

She was at a neighbor's house that was very close to ours. This neighbor was like family to us. We called her Granny. She was like a granny to every kid around. She was a voodoo doctor. She was known to treat children's sickness from the *lougarou* (witches) in the area. That night while she was trying to treat my mother's sickness, I was able to feel all the pain that my mother had to go through. The treatment included beating her with some special tree branches to beat the so-called zombie out of her. Oh, she was beaten over and over and over again! However, the so-called zombie never left because she only ever got sicker. I can still hear her pained voice screaming for help. I was only a child, weak and helpless. I could not have done anything, and no one else could have either. Only Jesus would have been able to save her! All she had to do was ask, but she did not know.

She went through so much, that poor lady! She never lived to see her children or grandchildren grow. She was young and beautiful, but she was weak, helpless, and fatherless. She wasn't even thirty years old when she died. I remember at her funeral, there was a singing group from my school that repeated an original song over and over that said, "*Souviens-toi que la terre est ta mère! Tu es poussière, tu retourneras a la poussière,*" which meant "Remember that the earth is your mother! You are dust, to dust you will return." How could I ever forget this song? It meant so much to me at the time. I was ten years old, and my younger brother, Wilner, was only seven. We were left motherless, and our dad was already living in the United States in order to help us financially and pay for our education.

CHAPTER TWO

My Father

My father, Molière Civil, was a very hard-working man. I never saw him sick when I was a child. He was healthy and strong. He was a man of few words who never got into trouble. He loved his children and worked hard to provide for us. I always enjoyed when he visited us in Haiti. He would bring little gifts for us and give me shiny coins: pennies, nickels, dimes, and quarters. When I took those shiny coins to the store, everyone knew that my father was home. I used to enjoy having him over.

He would sit me on his lap while listening to his beloved Haitian *bolero* and Haitian *méringue* dance music. He would spend hours sitting and listening to all these Haitian groups, such as Jazz des Jeunes, Orchestre Septentrional, and Orchestre Tropicana d'Haiti. He especially loved this beautiful song from Guy Durosier titled "*Ma Brune*." There was also a song he enjoyed called "*Fleur de Mai*." Jazz des Jeunes also performed it, and my dad enjoyed their version more than the original by Gérad Dupervil. He also loved this famous Haitian *méringue* called "*Chouboulout*," which had been performed by l'Orchestre Citadelle, as well as "*Si Tu Veux Gisel*," which was sung by Roger Colas from Septentrional. Maybe his love for the poetry and emotion in these songs is why I can never hold my tears when I hear them now.

> *My brothers and sisters and I had at least one thing in common: we were a bunch of motherless children! That's why we learned to have each other's back.*

My father had children with three different women who died early in their lives. I don't really know the cause of their death. I never saw him going to church, but he would wake up every morning and do the sign of the cross and recite his prayers facing the sun. Afterward, he would ask us how the night was and wouldn't say anything else unless he wanted us to go buy him something or do something for him. He was a man of few words! Regardless, my brothers and sisters and I had at least one thing in common: we were a bunch of motherless children! That's why we learned to have each other's back. That's why we learned to protect each other, to look after each other, to appreciate and love each other—because we only had each other.

My dad (seated) with my siblings and me.

CHAPTER THREE

My Siblings

Pierre-Richard

I remember back in kindergarten at *Sainte Thérèse de l'Enfant Jésus* when my older brother, Pierre-Richard, had to pick me up from school. He would carry me on his back and buy me fresco with *pistach* (scrunched ice with syrup and pistachios). That was so much fun! He was given money to pay for a *camionette* (public transportation), but he chose to carry me on his back when I got tired, and we enjoyed the money on fresco and *pistach* instead. Pierre-Richard was funny, loving, and caring. He always showed me that he loved me and always wanted to protect me. Even now, as adults, he always tells me that he is proud of the woman that I have become. I love him so much, and I am so blessed to have him as an older brother.

Gertha

My sister Gertha is my mother's age. Ironic, isn't it? She is beautiful and nice with a free spirit and does not take nonsense from people. She left home to go live in Martinique about the same time my dad left the country. I always liked it when she came to Haiti to see us. She always brought nice stuff and beautiful clothes for me. I remember when I was in my fourth year of secondary school, I was the only girl in my class wearing bows. My sister, Myrlène, never wanted to stop doing my hair as though I was still a little girl. I guess she didn't want me to grow up too fast. Gertha was the one who convinced her to perm my hair and let me look like a young lady. I was so happy to be free from wearing bows! I was always loved, cared for, and protected by her. I am so blessed to have been born in an unusual family where we learned to share love with one another. I never paid attention to the term "half-brothers" and "half-sisters." We were and are just brothers and sisters with the same father. We all have the same last name, lived in the same house, shared the same sorrows and happiness. Just like my brother

Wilner and I, we were all motherless children, for the previous mothers died just like my mom did.

Myrlène

My other older sister, Myrlène, whom my younger brother, Wilner, called, "*Manman* Myrlène," took responsibilities into her own hands to be the mother in the house when my mom died and Gertha wasn't around. Although Wilner called her mom, I never did. I never liked the fact that she made me do all the house chores when we didn't have a maid. Sometimes even with a maid, she still made me cook because she said a girl needs to learn how to cook in order to be ready for her husband, but Wilner never had to cook or do the chores. I hated being a girl because of that. Wilner was able to go in the neighborhood and play with his friends, but I had to stay home to cook, clean, and take care of the house. This cultural gender issue is not only in Haiti; it's all over the world. Although things have gotten better over the years, we still have a long way to go as a society. I loved my sister, but I hated the fact that she made me do all the work while my brother was having fun with his friends. She is just the result of a system that was made way before she was even born. I was so disgusted when she made me kill chickens to prepare for a nice Sunday meal. It was torture for me to cut the neck of the chicken—to actually take a knife and kill the poor animal! I felt like an assassin! Although I didn't like all the cooking back then, I am thankful to Myrlène now for teaching me how to cook. Nowadays, so many friends and family members enjoy my cooking. I even have a little cooking business called Veggie Delight because I enjoy cooking healthy food for my family and friends.

Francky

My brother, Francky, known as Fanfan, became my father after my father left Haiti to go find a better life. Fanfan was strict; he never let me go out and do certain things that most girls my age were doing. I was really afraid of him while growing up. However, I realized that was his way of protecting me from a lot of things that were going on. Francky was a loving father before he even became a father. He was loving, protective, and caring. One Saturday night, there were a bunch of armed men called "*attachés*," who were terrorizing the people of Bizoton, and they almost took me hostage. I was coming home from doing errands for my sister, Myrlène, in Diquini, and those armed men were coming toward me. I heard one of them say, "*Gade yon bèl ti grenn! Nou manje aswè a,*" which meant, "Look at that beautiful one! We have food for tonight!" As they were getting closer to me with their guns, I saw someone at my right open the door to let someone else come inside. I ran into this person's house as fast as I could and heard many gun shots behind me. I left the owner of the house in her living room and went straight to her bedroom and hid under her bed. The house belonged to a nice Christian family. They prayed and asked God to protect us, but Fanfan almost lost his life that night. The armed men almost found him in the street. While I was sleeping peacefully in their house, my brother Fanfan was in that terrorized street, trying to come to my rescue. They would probably have killed him that night if he hadn't found a place to hide. While he was hiding, there was a dog who saw him. The dog miraculously didn't even bark. In his attempts to rescue me, Fanfan did something heroic that many fathers wouldn't do for their own children! I love Fanfan! He is still a father figure to me!

On the Sunday morning that followed that tragic night, Myrlène asked me to cook breakfast, and I told her that I had a headache, and I was still in shock of what happened last night. Francky went down the big street to buy some *pate kòde* (Haitian patty) to eat. While he was there, the same group of armed men were beating people and taking them to prison for no reason whatsoever. One of them pointed his gun at Fanfan and said, "*Mare ke chemiz avèk misye*," which meant, "Tie your shirt with that other man who is right next to you." They went on to tell Fanfan, "You are going to pay for your arrogance." Although my brother didn't know what type of arrogance the armed man was talking about, he knew he had to do something to save his life. He waited until the armed man was terrorizing someone else and then ran as fast as he could in a muddy river. He never let go of his *pate kòde*, even when the man was shooting after him. Later, he learned that the young man with whom he was supposed to tie his shirt had been beaten almost to death and left paralyzed.

Nazaire

I was also loved by my brother, Nazaire, known as Ti Sonson. He was a loving and caring person. He was a tall, handsome man. From what I can remember, he was the one who I asked for money when I needed some. I remember one day I went to the place where he worked and asked him for money. He didn't have any. Instead of telling me he didn't have any, he borrowed it from his co-worker to give to me. He always said that he didn't want anyone to take advantage of me by giving me money. He told me not to take money from any man because they don't usually do it for free. He was always so happy to tell his friends that I am his little sister.

His favorite proverb was, "*Tout m'attire, rien ne m' attache*," which meant that "everything attracts me; nothing binds me." In other words, he was not attached to anything. He was easy to talk to and a great listener. He was always in the search of a better life. Unfortunately, he passed away without seeing his dream become a reality. He died after Wilner and I had already moved to the United States. On the day he died, I was at work and could not hold myself together. I was sad, weak, stressed, and overwhelmed without knowing why. Although I knew that he was sick, I didn't know that he died until I got home that day and my godmother, Marie Andrée, who I was living with in Brooklyn, gave me the news. I felt devastated, but when I heard that he gave his heart to Jesus before his death, I became hopeful because surely I will see my brother again one day! I will be able to hug him and praise the Lord together with him. Oh! When I go to heaven, what a day of rejoicing that will be! When I see my Jesus I will sing, praise, and shout HALLELUJAH! I will sing victory over pains, victory over sickness, victory over gender discrimination, victory over death! I know that I will see my dear brother again! You know why? The Bible tells me so!

> …He will swallow up death forever. The Sovereign LORD will wipe away the tears from all faces; he will remove his people's disgrace from all the earth. The LORD has spoken. (Isa. 25:8, NIV)

> Do not be amazed at this, for a time is coming when all who are in their graves will hear his voice and come out—those who have done what is good will rise to live, and those who have done what is evil will rise to be condemned. (John 5:28, 29, NIV)

> Behold, I shew you a mystery; we shall not all sleep, but we shall all be changed, in a moment, in the twinkling of an eye, at the last trump: for the trumpet shall sound, and the dead shall be raised incorruptible, and we shall be changed. For this corruptible must put on incorruption, and this mortal must put on immortality. So when this corruptible shall have put on incorruption, and this mortal shall have put on immortality, then shall be brought to pass the saying that is written, Death is swallowed up in victory. (1 Cor. 15:51–54, KJV)

> If ye then be risen with Christ, seek those things which are above, where Christ sitteth on the right hand of God. Set your affection on things above, not on things on the earth. For ye are dead, and your life is hid with Christ in God. When Christ, who is our life, shall appear, then shall ye also appear with him in glory. (Col. 3:1–4, KJV)

Brothers and sisters, we do not want you to be uninformed about those who sleep in death, so that you do not grieve like the rest of mankind, who have no hope. For we believe that Jesus died and rose again, and so we believe that God will bring with Jesus those who have fallen asleep in him. According to the Lord's word, we tell you that we who are still alive, who are left until the coming of the Lord, will certainly not precede those who have fallen asleep. For the Lord himself will come down from heaven, with a loud command, with the voice of the archangel and with the trumpet call of God, and the dead in Christ will rise first. After that, we who are still alive and are left will be caught up together with them in the clouds to meet the Lord in the air. And so we will be with the Lord forever. (1 Thess. 4:13–17, NIV)

The way the Bible explains it is that the wage of sin is death. But God, who alone is immortal, will grant eternal life to His redeemed. Eternal salvation is open to everyone; however, you must choose to accept it. God does not force anyone unto His kingdom. Everyone will have to make the choice to accept or reject it. Those who chose Him and are now in the grave are awaiting His return. Until that day, death is an unconscious state for all people. When Christ, who is life, appears, the resurrected righteous and living righteous will be glorified and caught up to meet their Lord. The second resurrection, the resurrection of the unrighteous, will take place a thousand years later.

"I know that my redeemer lives, and that in the end he will stand on the earth. And after my skin has been destroyed, yet in my flesh I will see God; I myself will see him with my own eyes—I, and not another. How my heart yearns within me!" (Job 19:25–27, NIV). Job declared that his eyes will see the Redeemer even when his flesh is destroyed.

"Do not put your trust in princes, in human beings, who cannot save. When their spirits depart, they return to the ground; on that very day their plans come to nothing" (Ps. 146:3, 4, NIV). The Bible clearly states that the dead know nothing. No more plans after death; no coming back to check on loved ones or hunt those they did not like while living. This is a false doctrine. This is spiritism. Satan himself is disguising himself in different ways to make us believe that the dead are still living and doing things around us.

For the living know that they shall die: but the dead know not any thing, neither have they any more a reward; for the memory of them is forgotten. Also their love, and their hatred, and their envy, is now perished; neither have they any more a portion for ever in any thing that is done under the sun…. Whatsoever thy hand findeth to do, do it with thy might; for there is no work, nor device, nor knowledge, nor wisdom, in the grave, whither thou goest. (Eccles. 9:5, 6, 10, KJV)

"Multitudes who sleep in the dust of the earth will awake: some to everlasting life, others to shame and everlasting contempt" (Dan. 12:2, NIV). The Bible is clear. There is nothing going on after death. We can sometimes dream about a loved one who passed away. That doesn't mean it is the spirit of the person who comes to us to give us advice or anything whatsoever. It is normal to dream about someone you love, even if the person is dead because we have great memories together.

I sometimes dream about my brother, Nazaire. He was a wonderful brother to me. A few years ago, the night before I traveled to Haiti for his son Efton's wedding, I saw Nazaire looking at me and smiling. For me, that dream was a normal dream. I know that my brother would have been so happy and approved of my actions. I was so happy to do something for his son. We can always dream about our loved ones after they are gone. It is normal for our loved ones to come to mind after they die. However, we should be careful about believing any or all the dreams we have because the devil can disguise himself in many ways to confuse people. When Jesus was talking about Lazarus, He explained that death is like a deep sleep:

After he had said this, he went on to tell them, "Our friend Lazarus has fallen asleep; but I am going there to wake him up." His disciples replied, "Lord, if he sleeps, he will get better." Jesus had been speaking of his death, but his disciples thought he meant natural sleep. So then he told them plainly, "Lazarus is dead…." (John 11:11–14, NIV)

Wilner

My younger brother, Wilner (Nènè), was quiet, sensitive, and loving. He and I grew up together. I am three years older than he is. We always took care of each other. I would cry every time he was getting spanked. He got baptized the same day I got baptized into the Adventist faith, but unfortunately, he left the faith. I don't know why. I am praying that he comes back and rededicates himself to the Lord. He is a hard-working man. He is in the Navy. He has been deployed many times. On one of his longer deployments, I lived in his house while I was planning to get my own house in Virginia where my husband and I and our three beautiful children now live.

Wilner loves my children, and my children love him so much. They are always praying for him. He never wants me to call him my little brother. He mostly acts like he's older than I am. I remember when we were kids, one night he was kicking really hard while sleeping, and he kept on saying "*Lage tifi a papa*" (Let go of the girl, man). He was really fighting hard that night. When he woke up in the morning, he told me what all the fighting and kicking was all about. In his dream he saw a young man who lives in our neighborhood pulling me to a corner, and he could tell I didn't like it because I was fighting back. He came and started to fight with the young man to try and protect me. My dear Nènè was always there for me. He loves music and likes the type of music that my dad used to listen to. He doesn't like to complain.

Wilner's favorite sentence is "I am good." He doesn't rely on others. He likes to work hard for what he wants. He joined the Navy at a very young age. I cried like a little baby when he went to boot camp. It was 5:00 in the morning. I gave him the best gift I had before he left; I gave him my Bible.

My brother, Wilner, and I.

While doing a devotional one morning, which was about the story of David and how God called him to become king, I couldn't stop thinking of Wilner. The youngest of the family. He was not the smartest nor the strongest while growing up, but the Lord used him to be a blessing for our family. The school system in Haiti did not do him justice. However, when we moved to the United States, he was doing so well that he was taking college statistics in high school. I think that he was not a good fit for the educational system in Haiti. He was the first one in the family to buy a house. He allowed me to live in his house for two years without paying any rent to help my husband and I save so that we could get our own house. My younger brother is one of the most courageous men that I know.

Although he is the youngest and was the least expected to be successful, God used him to teach us that we need to learn to see beyond what we see. We need to use words in a positive way and uplift one another. We need to speak greatness unto one another! We are blessed! We are protected! We are loved! We are beautiful! By the grace of God, we can accomplish greatness! By the grace of God, we can help those around us accomplish greatness! We can help someone in need of attention to know that he/she is loved, accepted, and appreciated! While he was at boot camp, we were only able to communicate through letters. I wrote him this poem titled, "To My Navy Brother."

To My Navy Brother

Wilner, my dear brother,
My love for you is even stronger
When I see you doing something better,
Something that can make you greater.

You chose the Navy and not the street
To prepare your future—that is so neat!
I don't know much about the Navy,
But you chose it, so for you I am happy.

All I am asking you is to stay focused.
No matter what happens, stay focused!
Think, act, and stay positive,
You will surely meet your objective!

To everyone always show respect,
You will probably not be the best,
But be the best you can be,
And success you will see!

Always give yourself a quiet time
Be grateful even with a single dime!
Remember to always pray,
Sing a song of praise every day!

Do every positive thing you can do today,
For you don't know if for you tomorrow will be a day!
Don't ever let anything make you go crazy,
And you will be a man full of dignity!

Many years later, I wrote this poem for Wilner's retirement from the military.

Retirement

Born on a beautiful day of Spring,
In our midst came one with the courage of a king.
Blessed with a wonderful heart that spreads love, compassion,
and selflessness,
You always shine as you strive always to offer to others your best.

My brother, you are one of a kind;
Your soul is golden and so kind.
Support for your family, you often find
As altruism is so deeply rooted in your mind.

You joined the Navy to make the family happy.
We cried! We prayed! And let you fly—
And watched you become all you could be.
We missed you many times, but as time flew by
Pride became ours, and we became happy you see.

Brave son of Haiti! Land of a Magnificent History!
You proudly became military
And leave a legacy for the Civil family.
Twenty-two years of hard work! We celebrate you!
As we praise God, our Shelter sure and true.

The devil had tried left and right, up and down,
To destroy, discredit, and put you down.
But Love Himself always came around;
By His rescuing arms, grace and mercy for you continue to abound.

We celebrate the GOD who has brought you through,
Strengthened you when your days were blue.
Wilner, the Lord has given you some great victories.
Cherish Him more than all the other memories.

We are proud of you! We love you!
We are part of you! Family blood, our forever glue.
See the fireworks in our eyes! We salute you.
Each time we meet again, a new sun will rise.

Wilner Civil! Congratulations on your retirement
As sweet victory becomes our melodious chant.

CHAPTER FOUR

Catholic! Were We?

As long as I could remember we called ourselves Catholic, but were we? I did my catechism and confessed my sins to the priest. The priest asked me for my sins, and I came up with something to get it over with. He did the sign of the cross and told me that my sins were forgiven. Did I believe him? No, I was too smart at that age, and I knew that it was just a formality. What sins was he saying were forgiven? Sins that I actually committed or the lies that I had to come up with to get through the process? The day of my first communion is so vivid in my mind. I was dressed in a beautiful white dress and white veil and crown. I had on white shoes—everything was white.

I felt so beautiful that day, and my dad took me to show respect to some family members after the service. When I got home, it was a big party with a lot of food and people. My cousins were there and kept on telling me how beautiful I was in my dress. Then there were my father's friends dancing to some Haitian *merengue* and *bolero*. They were happy, drunk, and hilarious! After my first communion, I only went to church once in a while. Inside the church were many statues that they call saints. I never remember praying to any of them. They were all weird to me. They all had biblical names in the Catholic church and different names in *tante* (aunt) Janita's *peristil* (voodoo temple). The exact same figures with different names. I heard that they had the same spirit behind them. I never understood why almost all of them were white, and they were called saints. However, when I started to read and study the Bible, I learned that the saints are those who choose to walk according to God's will. I began to realize that I can be called a saint. I became a saint through Jesus who died for me and cleansed me by His blood. The fact that I became a saint does not mean that people can pray to me and start calling me Saint Suzette! Romans 1:7 states, "To all those in Rome who are loved by God and called to be saints: Grace to you and peace from God our Father and the Lord Jesus Christ" (ESV). Also, in Revelation 14:12, it is said that, "Here is a call for the endurance of the saints, those who keep the commandments of God and their faith in Jesus" (ESV).

My Spiritual Journey

Before I get into my spiritual journey, let me share one of my poems with you.

The Touch

He touched me, oh! He touched me!
Have you ever been touched?
A special touch
A touch that makes you whole?
A touch that cleans your soul?

Have you ever been touched?
I mean, a deep touch!
That made you realize
Only Christ could
Your life normalize.

Have you ever been touched?
I'm talking about that special touch
That gets into your body and mind
And made you realize that you were blind
And could not see any divine sign.

Have you ever been touched?
By that Divine and penetrating touch?
And started to sing
"Amazing grace, how sweet the sound that saves a wretch like me!
I was once lost, but now am found,
Was blind, but now I see?!"

Oh brother! Oh sister! I have been touched
By that wonderfully Divine touch.

I was blind!
I was out of my mind!
Looking for a sign!
Looking for the Divine!

I was lost!
Sin, that is what I had the most.
Eternity was not on my list.
Sanctification, consecration were not in my midst.

In my search I found a woman
She said to me "I believe in God the Creator,
But Jesus is just a prophet, not our Redeemer,
and the Holy Spirit is just a force."

I stayed with that woman for a period of time
And realized that I still needed a sign.

I decided to continue my route
I found another woman, who likes to shout,
A woman with unusual songs
A woman who said she speaks in tongues.
A woman who calls herself pure,
But she loves money, attention, and leisure.

She said to me "I believe in God, the Creator.
I accept Jesus as my Savior,
And the Holy Spirit is my conductor.
I can praise the Lord any day!
I can worship my Creator any and every day."

Oh! I started to let that woman lead me!
I started to let her teach me!
I started to let her feed me!
Oh! I started to let her take me
Until one day the Holy Spirit touched me
And delivered me from my blindness
And took me out of my darkness
In order to lead me to holiness.

Oh! He touched me
And enlightened me
Oh! He touched me
And sanctified me
Oh! He touched me with the touch that brings perfect glee.

Those women I talked about in my poem are different churches that I have encountered in my spiritual journey. The Bible describes churches as women. In Bible prophecy, a woman represents a church. The pure virgin woman is the church of God. The harlot, the adulteress is the apostate church who had given herself to the kings and princes of this world. Since after the first sin in the garden of Eden, the Lord said to the serpent, "And I will put enmity between you and the woman, and between your seed and her Seed; He shall bruise your head, and you shall bruise His heel" (Gen. 3:15, NKJV). The battle against the church, the pure woman, started right in Eden.

In 2 Corinthians 11:2, we can see God is jealous for His wife, the church: "For I am jealous over you with godly jealousy: for I have espoused you to one husband, that I may present you as a chaste virgin to Christ" (KJV). It is said in Revelation 12:1, "And there appeared a great wonder in heaven; a woman clothed with the sun, and the moon under her feet, and upon her head a crown of twelve stars" (KJV). Revelation 19:7 also mentions the woman in a positive way and invites everyone to join their celebration. "Let us be glad and rejoice, and give honour to him: for the marriage of the Lamb is come, and his wife hath made herself ready" (KJV).

As the beautiful wife is making herself ready, the harlot is making herself rich by committing adultery with the kings and princes of this world.

> The woman was arrayed in purple and scarlet, and adorned with gold and precious stones and pearls, having in her hand a golden cup full of abominations and the filthiness of her fornication. And on her forehead a name *was* written: MYSTERY, BABYLON THE GREAT, THE MOTHER OF HARLOTS AND OF THE ABOMINATIONS OF THE EARTH. I saw the woman, drunk with the blood of the saints and with the blood of the martyrs of Jesus. And when I saw her, I marveled with great amazement. (Rev. 17:4–6, NKJV)

This harlot is drunk with the blood of the saints and the martyrs of Jesus Christ. This woman is none other than the one who has persecuted God's church for centuries. She is a church that has committed adultery with the authorities of this world. She is rich and has been drunk by the blood of the servant of God, the blood of the martyrs.

I believe that during my search, God was already there with me step by step on the way to salvation. He is the way, the truth, and the light. I was looking for the light, but the light was there reaching for me. I just needed to surrender to Him. I had numerous unanswered questions that I needed to clarify.

One day, on my way home from school, a man who I had always seen in the store lent me a religious book to read. I was probably thirteen or fourteen years old. When I read that book, it made no sense to me whatsoever. It was about an angel named Moroni who helped a man find a prophetic book. That man became a prophet, and the story went on, but I didn't care for it at all.

Then I started to have Bible studies with a young man whose group usually went to people's homes and told them about the kingdom of heaven. The Bible study went well, but the Bible teacher never prayed with me before the lesson. He only started praying with me after he taught me the way they themselves pray. I even visited their services a couple of times. I found them to be really educated, but I didn't find actual spirituality amongst them.

One summer, a friend invited me to a Sunday afternoon church service. They had a nice youth program. The following Sunday I went again, and I even had a solo in a song called "El Shaddai," which I had practiced throughout the week. I still remember the lyrics, but I sang the French version, of course, because I didn't speak English at that time. The only English I knew was only a little bit of what I learned in school. On

> *I was looking for the light, but the light was there reaching for me.*

the following Sunday, a neighbor invited me to the church where the pastor was also the director of my school. I really liked that church. Some of the leaders there were my teachers at school as well. I got baptized there and was a member of a singing group, which I enjoyed immensely. The other members were so nice. We not only spent time practicing songs but we also prayed and fasted together. I really felt loved, accepted, and respected. The name of the group was, "*Les Enfants d'ELOÏM*" (The Children of Elohim). I still communicate with many of the members of this group. I think back fondly to the great moments we shared. The love and the profound level of humility I found in these other young people was exceptional. I can't recall one day where any bad incident happened in this group. It was a blessing for me to be part of that wonderful group. I still love them. It was so hard for me to leave this group and that church when I received two revelations from God about a biblical truth that I didn't know.

One night, I was dreaming, and I saw an Adventist young man named Emanuel, who lived in my neighborhood in Bizoton, preaching to me about the Sabbath. He told me that the Sabbath is still important to God, and He wants all His children to observe it. I told him in the dream the same thing I usually told every Adventist person who wanted to convince me about the Sabbath. I talked about Galatians 3:24, 25. These used to be my favorite verses to use against the Adventists. Here they are! "Wherefore the law was our schoolmaster to bring us unto Christ, that we might be justified by faith. But after that faith is come, we are no longer under a schoolmaster" (KJV). Boom! I was so proud of myself for knowing the right verse to close his mouth about the Sabbath, but he only calmly told me that Jesus did not come to abolish the law and the prophets. He came to accomplish what the ceremonial law was not able to do. He told me that the ceremonial law was the one that Jesus accomplished at the cross. He is the Lamb of God that came to save us from sin. The law, the schoolmaster's job, was to bring us to Christ. Christ has come; we do not have to kill any lamb or make any sacrificial ceremony for the forgiveness of our sins anymore.

In my dream, that young Adventist man convinced me about the Sabbath. I woke up and said to myself, *Why did I ever let an Adventist convince me in my dream? I will never let that happen when I am awake! Anyway, they don't even know what they are talking about.* After that dream, I continued going to my church like nothing really happened. I still enjoyed my singing group and went singing with my friends many Sunday mornings and afternoons. Wherever we received an invitation to sing, I happily accompanied the group and enjoyed the love we were getting from pastors, members, and people in the community. I still attended my church on Sunday morning and participated in all worship services. I was really comfortable at my church and did not have any intention to leave for a bunch of people that I found weird, arrogant, and who had no clue about the Bible!

> *In my dream, that young Adventist man convinced me about the Sabbath. I woke up and said to myself, Why did I eve, let an Adventist convince me in my dream? I will never let that happen when I am awake! Anyway, they don't even know what they are talking about.*

In January of 1995, a friend named Herby invited me to attend a Revelation seminar at his Adventist church. At first, I told him no, but he insisted and kept on inviting me over and over again. I finally said yes and that I would go the next day. That night I went to sleep just fine with nothing bothering me, but when I woke up, my body was full of hives everywhere from my face to my feet. They looked like a very bad allergic reaction to something that I don't know. My body was so itchy that I couldn't keep any clothes on. When my friend came to take me to the service, I had to tell one of my siblings to tell him that I can't come. I was not even able to go tell him myself. He said he would come the next day. The next day I woke up with a bad diarrhea that made me spend a lot of time in the bathroom. When Herby came to take me, I told him that I can't go because I am sick with diarrhea. He told me, "My friend, you need to go. I am going to find you a seat next to a bathroom if you have to go during the service." I agreed because I felt guilty of not keeping my promise.

That first night I went, the pastor was preaching about God's moral law, the Ten Commandments. He declared that God wrote the Ten Commandments with His own hands twice. I was amazed by that truth that I never knew was in the Bible even though I thought I knew so much. I soon realized how little biblical knowledge I had. Pastor Sylveus Victor went on and said that Moses broke the first Ten Commandments stone, and God met with him on the mountain again and wrote the Ten Commandments with His own fingers. He said this law was never abolished, and Christ never took away the Ten Commandments that represented the character of God. To my surprise, I did not even need to take one single trip to the bathroom. I realized it was the enemy's tricks to stop me from going and listening to God's word.

Around that same time, I had another dream that terrified me. In my dream, I was coming home from school and was stopped by a very tall man who stopped me at a gas station between my school and an Adventist church named Morijah. When I saw him, I was so afraid that I was shaking. The man in the dream had a bat in his hand and was trying to hit me. He told me with a rage, "Don't go! I need you to come and serve me." As I was approaching him, a force came over me, and I told him bravely, "*Au nom de Jésus map sove!*" Which means "In the name of Jesus, I will be saved!" The man was so mad that he threw away his bat and left. Then I continued walking until I stopped in front of the Adventist church. I was then preaching to some Adventist young ladies who were at my school and were members at that church. These young ladies did not carry a good testimony of God by the way they carried themselves at school. I saw myself preaching to them about the way they needed to live as Christians. I told them they needed to observe the Sabbath of the Lord truly or stop pretending they were Adventists when deep down inside, they were worse than those who don't know the truth. When I woke up from that dream, I was convinced that God wanted me to become a Seventh-day Adventist, and Satan was trying so hard to stop me. I was and am so happy that Jesus gave me victory.

I continued to go to the evangelistic series every night. One of my friends who used to be in my prayer group from my previous church got baptized, and my other friend, Dieulande, also got baptized. However, I was still thinking, *What I am going to do? Where am I going to eat? My family eats pork, and I have nowhere else to eat.* I said to myself, *I can't become an Adventist. I have to eat what is cooked at home, and my sister told the maid to still cook pork, and I have no right to ask what is in the food because I don't work. I have to eat whatever is served.*

That night, I went to the service. I was so shocked when the pastor was talking about things that I was only saying in my heart. He said, "Why are you worrying yourself about what you should eat? Don't you know that God who created everything can take care of you?" The pastor was pointing right at me, and I felt that his eyes were looking at me. I was shaking in my seat. Tears were coming down my cheeks. That night I stood and decided that I was going to get baptized regardless of what my siblings, who were actually my parents, said. My younger brother, Wilner, decided to get baptized as well.

> *I was convinced that God wanted me to become a Seventh-day Adventist, and Satan was trying so hard to stop me. I was and am so happy that Jesus gave me victory.*

There was a lot of tension at home when we made that decision. The older siblings didn't want us to get baptized into the Adventist church. My older sister who used to take care of us asked, "Who is going to do your Saturday chores for you? You know that Saturday is one of the busiest days in this house. It is clean-up day; you can't go to church when everybody will be cleaning and cooking and get ready for Sunday." Culturally, Sunday was the day we had a nice, big dinner. We usually started the preparation for it on Saturday. Although we had a maid at that time, I was supposed to help with the preparation.

The tension got so bad that the morning I was supposed to get baptized, I had decided in my heart to just give up this idea of going and getting baptized and becoming a member of the Adventist church. A man who had nothing to do with the church named Ti Gana came and asked me why I was still home and why wasn't I getting ready to go get baptized. I believe that God sent him that morning to tell me that I better go. This unexpected messenger vividly exemplified that God has the power to use even a rock to talk if human beings are not willing to talk. That man was a rock that God was using that morning to tell me to go get baptized. While I was at the church that Sabbath, I heard that one of my older brothers came, and he was really mad at the pastor and told the pastor if he baptized me or my younger brother, he would light the church on fire. The pastor came and told me that my brother was there and was furious about the baptism decision. I said that I was going to get baptized anyway, and I did.

> *Although things were hard, the Lord never left us alone. He provided in many ways.*

After the baptism, we couldn't go home. My brother said we were no longer part of the family and that the pastor should consider adopting me and my younger brother. It took all the church elders and some deacons to take us home. Among the elders was Elder Wilfrid Louis Jean, who is now a pastor. My brother was furious. There were many people talking and telling my brother to stay firm on his decision. Some said that it was very disrespectful of us to make such a decision. Some said that Adventism is the worst religion of all. Even neighbors who had nothing to do with our decision making had something to say. I felt like everybody was judging us—except one woman named Nicole who said she wished that her kids would make that same decision instead of following the pleasures of the world. That nice woman was the only person who said something positive that day. Everyone else was talking about us like we had just committed a crime that couldn't be forgiven. I looked into my older brother's eyes; they were red with rage. He was so angry and didn't even want to accept us into our father's home. My brother, who had so much love and was willing to risk his own life to save me from the gunmen a few years before, was not even looking at us as family anymore. The enemy was using him to get back at us for making the decision to walk with Jesus.

Although things were hard, the Lord never left us alone. He provided in many ways. I was able to eat at the school restaurant every day for a while and paid monthly with the money that my father had decided to send directly to me from the United States. I was so thankful that he decided that I should have my own money every month. I was worried about where I was going to eat, but God had provided before I even asked Him to do so. With that little money that my father was sending for me every month, I was not totally dependent on my sister for food. My friend, Dieulande, was also a great support to me. She fed me when I didn't have money and didn't want to eat pork at home. Even rice and beans were cooked with pork! Anyway, I was so blessed to have food to eat when I couldn't eat at home. My sister's husband eventually convinced her to stop cooking with pork to be healthier, and then I was able to eat at home with no problem again.

I spent a year as a member of Morijah before I came to the United States. I used to participate in every church activity. Every Tuesday was prayer and fasting day. One Tuesday, I decided to stay home to wash my clothes. While I was doing so, I was singing and praising God. Then a stranger came asking for me. He said he had an important letter for me. It was my immigration letter. He said he didn't know how my letter was mailed to his address because I lived far from where he lived. When I opened the letter, it said that I needed to be in the United States before I turned twenty-one . I had to go to the US embassy to meet with the consulate. I took the form to school and had my English teacher help me fill it out. Eventually, every procedure that needed to be done was done, and my father sent the ticket for me to come to the United States and live in the country of opportunities.

CHAPTER FIVE

Arrival in the United States

In the cold winter of February 1996, I arrived in Brooklyn, New York. My father and cousin, Mirlène, came to pick me up at the JFK International Airport. I was so happy to be in the United States with my father. I spent the night at the house he was living in with my cousins and my Aunt Germaine, his sister. The next day he had to take me to Marraine's (my godmother) house because there was not enough space at my aunt's house for me.

I was so blessed to go live with Marraine Marie Andrée. She was and still is a beautiful woman inside and out. Among all the mothers that God put on my path to mold me into the woman that I am today, she is one of them! She always shows me love, respect, and support. She is also a very funny woman. She always has some jokes up her sleeve that would make you laugh so hard that your cheeks hurt. There is so much laughter at her house. Her son, Marc-Fallen, with whom I grew up in Haiti, also sees me as family. Yes, we are family! Family doesn't require blood. We just need to accept, respect, and love one another! I love her daughter Stephanie as well, and I am so proud of the young woman she has become. I used to do her hair and take her to elementary school. Marraine's husband, Jean Mary, even treats me like a daughter. They are wonderful people! I love them!

One thing Marraine used to tell me often is "*Suze ou pa kite pitit Haïti; se pou ou al lekòl; aprann yon bagay pou lavi w; se pa chita ap travay sèlman*," which translates to, "Suze, you didn't leave any children in Haiti; you need to go to school, do something with your life; don't just work and work." She would continue and tell me she wished she had been as young as I was when I came to the United States because she would have loved to go to college and learn something. She was always so happy when I accomplished something. I used to love the smile on her face when she was telling people "*Se fiyèl mwen*" (This is my goddaughter) when she introduced me to them.

I remember there was a young lady in the building where we lived who was working at the same place I was working. That young lady was jealous of me because the manager who was also Haitian was nice to me. She used to dress with very short and tight dresses to get attention. Unfortunately, she didn't get the attention she was seeking from the manager. He used to like coming to my table to start a conversation about literature or history—always something intellectual. He used to tell me that I was an intelligent young lady, and I needed to go to school. The young lady was so mad that she went and told almost everyone at work that I was having an affair with the manager who was a married man. That day I went home crying. Marraine took me to the young lady's apartment and asked for her mother. She seriously and proudly said to them that "*Suze pat vinn isit pou li pran mari moun*," meaning, "Suze didn't come here to steal other people's husbands." She went on to say, "Her goal is to go to college and do something with herself. Don't fool yourself if you can't get the man; it's not Suze's fault."

The next day, I went to work, and that young lady couldn't even look me in the eyes. I am so glad that God put Marraine Marie Andrée in my life. She was able to not only stop that young lady's rumors but she also boosted my confidence, and she pushed me to go to college. I love you, Marraine! Only God can pay you back for all that you have done for me! Please give your life to Jesus! I hope to see you in heaven!

My First Sabbath in the United States

In that cold winter of February 1996, I woke up early and was happy to go to church for my first Sabbath in the United States. I put on my nice clothes, but I was not happy to put a coat on top of it. I felt very different wearing such a heavy thing on. However, when I left the building to get in the car of the person who picked me up, I was so grateful to have a coat. I felt like I was about to lose my ears because I didn't want to wear the things Marraine gave me to cover my ears. That Sabbath, the youth of that church were celebrating Black History Month. I had no clue something like that even existed. The music was loud! The choir was loud! The preacher was super loud! The youngsters were singing and dancing on the stage. I was so shocked to see such a manifestation inside an Adventist church. When I got home, I told Marraine all about it. Although she did not know about Adventist churches in Brooklyn, she called one of her friends who was an Adventist to ask about a good Haitian Adventist church. The friend told her about Gethsemane and gave us the address. The following Sabbath I went to Gethsemane.

Gethsemane

My first Sabbath at Gethsemane was wonderful and welcoming. The service was exactly like the type of services that I am used to in Haiti. The Sabbath School teacher was nice and knowledgeable. There, I met a friend who I knew in Haiti, Samuel Michel. He became like a big brother to me. He was the one who introduced me to everyone. He also was the one to take me to register for evening courses at Prospect High School to get ready for college. He would ask me to do presentations during our Sabbath School class. Before I knew it, I was asked to help during Sabbath School, and I eventually became a Sabbath School teacher for the children of the church. I really enjoyed teaching the children, and I also learned from older teachers such as Sister Blanc, who we called *Sœur* Cocotte, and Sister Guerda. Soon, I was asked to be the children's ministries leader and, finally, the Adventurer's leader. I enjoyed every moment teaching these children.

At Gethsemane, I was blessed to have some wonderful mothers, sisters, fathers, and brothers. This is the church that helped me grow spiritually, intellectually, and socially. I am so blessed that I was never alone. The Lord always put wonderful people in my life. This world is full of marvelous people and things created by the Creator for our happiness. I was in a new land, meeting new people, learning a new language, yet I didn't feel lonely and sad. If you ever feel lonely, look around you, and you will realize that you are never alone. Let me share another poem with you.

I Will Never Be Alone

I will never be alone anymore
For the universe is my home
I choose not to be alone in my life
For God is by my side.

I will not be alone in this world
Because in the beginning was the Word
This Word became man to save me
From sin, deliver me.

How could I be alone when I wake up
And see the sun that helps me stay up
When I see people passing by my way
So many faces I can see day by day!

Some look nice, some look even nicer
Some look happy, some look sad
Some are smiling, others are laughing!
Some are rejoicing, some are crying!

I can't be alone when I look at the sky
I see different birds fly by and by
Some are colorful, some white, black
But they are all together on track!
In their songs there is harmony!
I feel blessed to hear their melody.
Their diversity and togetherness make me happy
What a symphony!!!

How could I be alone when I know my Jesus cares
And my brothers and sisters are there to share!
To share wisdom when life is unfair
And remind me that God is there!

How could I be alone in my life
When there is a beautiful child
Who is asking for attention
Who is in need of compassion!

I will never be alone anymore
Because I have God's big and small blessings for comfort
Everything to bring me happiness
Everything, yes, everything in the universe!

I wrote this poem one day when I felt lonely and decided to change my state of mind. I wanted to cry and decided to count God's blessings instead. Gethsemane was my place to go when things were cloudy and shakable. I was always there. Tuesday morning for prayer and fasting; Wednesday night for prayer meeting; Saturday was usually an all-day long affair; and Sunday morning was for Pathfinder and Adventurer club with my friend and sister, Jocelyn Menard. We used to always be together. She is truly a sister that the Lord gave me who was and still is always there when I need her. I love you, Jo! She truly cares about me and has helped me in many ways. She was so happy for me when I graduated college, and I was happy for her as well when she graduated. She is a book-smart person. She always got A's and was an honor student. I was so happy to be invited to her pinning ceremony.

She likes to cook fancy dinners. I remember every time she invited me to one of her fancy dinners, I would always make sure I ate a little something before I went because I know when she says fancy, she usually takes her time to make sure that everything is perfect. The plates, the cups, the napkins, and the utensils would be arranged in a way that was fit for a king. She would even have candles. Yes, a candle dinner just for me and her. She didn't need a special occasion to have a candlelight dinner. She just made ordinary moments special. She would follow all the table etiquette rules and take her time with every bite. I had to follow along and take my time as well. Everything, from the salad to the dessert, was exquisitely delicious! Jocelyn is so funny, but only people who are close to her will know this side of her. She is very sensitive and loving even though she seems so strict and firm. She is a prayer warrior, and she is one of my prayer partners.

On Sabbath morning, I usually wake up early to be on the Sabbath School prelude. At 9:30 a.m., it was time for Sabbath School. Right after that, it was time for lay ministry, usually led by sister Ismaël, who would start by saying "*Laïques de Gethsemane!*" (Laymen of Gethsemane!) And the people would answer, "*Toujours prêts!*" (Always ready!) When she had the microphone, everyone was awake! She was a powerful preacher. Everyone called her *Sœur* Mama. The lay ministry announcements were done by a well-spoken and beautiful lady named Fabienne. She was always nicely dressed; I admired her style. The worship service was very meticulous! The pastor, the elders, and one woman usually conducted it. I always enjoyed the services, except when there was a nominations committee.

After the service, some of us would stay and have lunch together. After we ate, we would have Bible study preparation class to get us ready to go preach and study the Bible with others. I always liked the way my dear brother, Delore, presented the study. He would take time to answer all doctrinal questions clearly with details. By the time I was done with the series, I felt ready to go study with others. Soon after we had finished that series, a young lady named Yvette came who wanted to study the Bible. She was about my age, and I was asked to conduct the Bible study along with an older man named George. Before we even finished the study, Yvette asked to get baptized. She did get baptized and became an active member of the church and one of my friends and sisters. She was the one who took me to Medgar Evers College and helped me fill out my application. It wasn't long before I was in college. Many wonderful people helped me with my college education.

Many people helped me through my journey. For instance, I am so grateful for a wonderfully intelligent man named Louis-Carl Saint Jean, who was there for me when I needed help. He enjoyed pushing people to be the best they can be academically. He often says, "*Je ne digère pas ceux qui veulent rester dans l'ignorance*," which means, "I can't tolerate those who choose to be ignorant." He is sometimes tough with his remarks, but I love him for his educated thoughts on culture and literature! He is someone who really took time to ask me how I am doing in school. He would say "*Si tu as besoin d'aide, n'hésite pas de m'appeler*" (If you need help, feel free to call me). I could call him anytime, and he was always happy to help. I still call him when I need him to look over a new poem I write or other things concerning culture, music, and, especially, Haitian literature and music. This man is a living encyclopedia. He even took time to come to my college to help me prepare for my exit writing exam before graduation. Many students, including me, were worrying about that exam because you must pass it to graduate. He taught me how to write my essay, and I was blessed to be among those who passed and were ready for graduation. Louis-Carl is a man of literature, culture, poetry, and good music. He always says things as they are, and I am blessed to call him my friend!

CHAPTER SIX

Prayer

There were wonderful people and prayer warriors filled with the Holy Spirit at Gethsemane that God used to help me through my journey. I remember that I was having difficulties passing my entrance writing exam for college. I took the test many times and couldn't get a passing grade. One Sabbath afternoon, the Sabbath School ministry team was having a prayer meeting. and the leader of that ministry, who was Sister Janine Joanie at that time, asked if anyone had a prayer request. I raised my hands and said, "Please pray for me so that I can pass my entrance writing exam." There were mostly older ladies there. They formed a circle, asked me to get in the middle, and fervently prayed for me. Afterwards, I had a dream that night. In my dream I was taking the test and was able to see what the essay was about. In that same dream, I saw that I passed the test. When I woke up the next day, I made sure I told my tutor to focus on that essay prompt, which was one of the ones in the list of essays we were working on in my ESL class. I wrote and rewrote that specific essay question many times.

On the day of the test, I felt prepared, confident, and blessed. I felt even more relaxed and excited when I saw the essay question I'd seen in my dream as one of the essay questions in the test. Without any doubt, I chose it and started to write after a short prayer in my heart. Usually when I was doing the test, I was never able to have enough time to finish. On that specific day, one of my victory days, I was able to finish before the time was up. I had time to go over my writing and check for grammatical errors. Then when I checked my result afterwards, I was so happy and blessed to see that I had passed. I was so excited to be able to move ahead with my college education. I praise God for different prayer groups that help keep the prayer light on. There is power in prayer. I love that hymn about prayer titled, "Sweet Hour of Prayer."

"Sweet hour of prayer, sweet hour of prayer,
That calls me from a world of care,
And bids me, at my Father's throne,
Make all my wants and wishes known!
In seasons of distress and grief,
My soul has often found relief,
And oft escaped the tempter's snare,
By Thy return, sweet hour of prayer.
Sweet hour of prayer! sweet hour of prayer!
The joys I feel, the bliss I share
Of those whose anxious spirits burn
With strong desires for Thy return
With such I hasten to the place
Where God my Savior shows His face
And gladly take my station there
And wait for Thee, sweet hour of prayer
Sweet hour of prayer
Sweet hour of prayer
And wait for Thee
Sweet hour of prayer"

Prayer moves mountains. It is a direct conversation with God. No need to go through any other channels to get to our heavenly Father. We just need to call Him in the name of Jesus, and He answers. In Philippians 4:5–7, it is said:

> Let your reasonableness be known to everyone. The Lord is at hand; do not be anxious about anything, but in everything by prayer and supplication with thanksgiving let your requests be made known to God. And the peace of God, which surpasses all understanding, will guard your hearts and your minds in Christ Jesus. (ESV)

2 Chronicles 7:14 is as follows, "If my people, who are called by my name, will humble themselves and pray and seek my face and turn from their wicked ways, then I will hear from heaven, and I will forgive their sin and will heal their land" (NIV).

Pray when everything is fine, and pray when the world seems to be upside down. Pray during happy moments; pray during deep sorrow. Keep on praying no matter what and how things turn out to be. We should never, ever stop praying.

Ephesians 6:18 presents prayer in a very easy to understand way: "And pray in the Spirit on all occasions with all kinds of prayers and requests. With this in mind, be alert and always keep on praying for all the Lord's people" (NIV).

Prayer must be a constant thing. A servant of God who needs to develop a relationship with Him needs to be constantly praying. Pray when everything is fine, and pray when the world seems to be upside down. Pray during happy moments; pray during deep sorrow. Keep on praying no matter what and how things turn out to be. We should never, ever stop praying. I am so grateful for all the prayer partners that God put on my path. If I said that I was born knowing how to pray, you would know that I am definitely lying to you, but if I told you that the Lord has put people, circumstances, the Bible, and other biblical books in my life to help me learn how to pray, please believe me. I am not talking for myself, but to praise the Lord my God for shaping my prayer life. I know that I am not where I need to be yet, but I am so happy that God is with me every step of the way to mold me into the person He wants me to be.

CHAPTER SEVEN

Medgar Evers College

What can I say about Medgar Evers College? In the summer of 1998, two years after being in the States, my friend, Yvette Remfort, took me there to fill out an admission application. A few weeks later, I was so happy when I received the admission letter. I felt special, blessed, and privileged of the honor of attending college. At Medgar Evers College, I learned more than academic courses. I learned about the struggles of black people in America. One day in an African American history class, I was so angry that I had to go and pray and ask the Lord to take away all that anger. I was so mad to see the way that Medgar Evers was murdered just for being born black and insisting on fighting for the right of education for all. He was murdered for propagating the beautiful truth that all men and women are created equal. They hated him for that. They wanted to keep the African Americans in ignorance, in poverty, in slavery. On Wednesday, June 12, 1963, after returning from a NAACP meeting, Medgar Evers was shot. He was shot in the back, and the bullet went through his heart. His wife, Myrlie found him in front of the front door. He was taken to a local hospital, but he died there thirty minutes later.

They murdered this courageous man of God for his advocacy for truth, equality, and true freedom for all. They murdered him in front of his home and didn't give him the opportunity to hug his wife and children one last time. He couldn't have dinner with his family that night. His wife was left to do the job of being a mother and a father for her children. This was the case for many prominent African American families back then. They murdered him the same way they murdered Martin Luther King Jr., Malcolm X, and so on. Even now, murder rates for African American men are disproportionately high compared to the rest of the American population. Oh, please stop the blood shedding. Stop the killing of those beautiful children of God. Don't you understand that the blood in our veins is the same color? Don't you understand how beautiful it is when we are together? When we are peacefully and lovingly working for the attainment of liberty and justice for all? This is our pledge of allegiance! Yes, one nation under God, with liberty and justice for all! When we all have liberty, when we all have justice, we can live harmoniously as brothers and sisters in this beautiful land of liberty. Below is a poem that I wrote as I thought through this issue.

We Are the Same

Why are you afraid of me?
You close your eyes and don't want to see.
Why do you close your heart and don't want to feel?
You kill your soul and don't want to dream.

Why do we have to be apart,
And don't want to open our hearts?
Why do we have to be so mean
When we can be very nice and clean?

Why can't we sit side by side
To contemplate together the color of the sky,
Feel the wind that caresses our skin,
And sing the liberty hymn!

Why don't we sing together
The song of love and harmony?
Why don't we talk together
The language of peace and unity?

Why don't we sing the pledge of allegiance
And burn away our indifference?
Why don't we sing "The Star-Spangled Banner"
And keep liberty and justice as forefront banners!!

While I was at Medgar Evers, I encountered some wonderful professors who went beyond teaching. They taught with love and passion. At Medgar Evers College, I learned not to be afraid to speak a language that I didn't know how to speak. My first ESL professor told me not to be afraid to express myself in English. Not to be ashamed of my accent. She even took the whole class to the Statue of Liberty for a field trip and told us that we all belong here because America is a country of immigrants. She said that no one should ever make us feel like we don't belong here. She looked at me and said, "Did you know that Haitian soldiers helped fight for our independence?" I was in disbelief of the fact that I didn't know this very important piece of Haitian history. She said there is a monument honoring these soldiers in Savannah, Georgia. I learned later that more than 500 Haitian free blacks joined American colonists and French troops in trying to drive the British away from coastal Savannah, Georgia.

The Haitian Monument in Savannah, Georgia.

This mural is located in an area with many Haitian immigrants.

CHAPTER EIGHT

Love

At Medgar Evers College, I also found love. One day while taking an exam, my heart felt strongly for a young man who was one of the supervisors of the exam. I was so into him that I didn't even realize that my time was almost coming to an end, and I didn't complete my exam. I had seen him before, and someone introduced him to me, so I found out his name was Heandel Noel, but I was not able to admire his masculine beauty until that day. I was impressed by the way he approached people who asked for help. When his beautiful brown eyes caught mine, I was already trembling from the inside. My heart was beating so fast that I felt like the person sitting next to me could have heard it. That day I was sure that I was in love with him. I melted when I heard his sweet voice. I was sure that I wanted to hear that voice over and over again. It was like a beautiful melody in my ear.

The next time I noticed him was in front of the Bedford building at Medgar Evers College. He had on a black pair of pants and a beautiful shirt with flowers. He looked so handsome, and he noticed me and came to say, "*Salut, comment ça va?*" (Hi, how are you?).

"*Je vais bien!*" (I am fine), I replied, with a smile on my face. After that, we couldn't stop talking to each other. We exchanged phone numbers and started to spend hours on the phone. It was during our long romantic hours on the phone that we realized that we both share a love for poetry. He started to write for me. I started to write for him. We were madly in love with each other. I wouldn't go to sleep without hearing his melodious voice telling me, "*Fais de beaux rêves, mon amour*" (Have wonderful dreams, my love). The poems we wrote to each other were mostly in French. Let me share this rare English one I wrote when he went to spend two weeks in Boston during summer vacation. I missed him so much and couldn't wait for him to come back.

I Miss You

It has been almost two weeks
That my heart is feeling sick
It seems like an eternity
Since I last saw my baby.

An eternity that our lips
Haven't joined on our trips
Trips to the city of love and happiness
Where there is no pain, no stress!

It has been so long
Without the harmony of our songs
The songs that our bodies make,
When together they are awake!

I miss your charming smile,
The silent conversation of our eyes.
I miss the tender expression of your face
And the way you always look at me.
I miss you
Yes, I miss you!

We became inseparable. We started to register for the same courses. We enjoyed studying together. We spent hours at the school library studying, but we also took quick breaks to go enjoy some quiet time outside. We would hold hands going in and out of the school. We never got tired of each other. Oh, I loved those beautiful moments with my friend, my love, my prayer partner. I praise God every day for my precious treasure. Oh, how I love this man, my man! He is the love of my life! He wrote some beautiful poems for me. One of them is this beautiful one utilizing my name titled, "Sweet Love."

Sweet Love

Sure, I love you dear honey
uncomparable is your beauty, your personality
zenith is where you often take me with your angelic voice!
Empty, my life would be without you

Tenderness is what you personify
Thy love is the most wonderful thing I could ever have.
Exhilarated I feel when I am in your arms!

Charming princess
Irresistibly and constantly, you charm me
Very dear you are to me
Incredible you are with all the sweetness you have
Love you with all of my heart sweety!

What does a young lady want more than a charming young man who is completely devoted to her, who treats her like a princess, and makes her feel that she is worth more than a million? He not only captured my heart with his charming self but we also shared the love of poetry. We didn't need a special occasion to write poems for each other. He didn't need a special reason to bring me flowers. He would bring me flowers just to say, "I love you." I prefer it that way. He didn't wait for Valentine's Day to bring me chocolate. He knows that I love chocolate, so he would just buy me some on his way to my house. Besides spending a lot of time together, we took pictures together. Everyone who entered my room when I was in college would notice his pictures all over my walls, my dresser, my closet door, by my bed—everywhere. We were definitely madly in love! We have written so many poems for each other and continue to do so. The majority of them are in French and Creole. Another English one Heandel wrote for me in 2004 is called, "My Love."

My Love

My love for you is authentic
As clarity is to noon
My heart presses to give you all its affection
That you yourself put in it with passion!

Happy to be the solar reflection that makes you, pretty diamond, shine
You are the treasure of treasures, so distinct, so fine
Your immense tenderness is the shadow that keeps our love fresh
Your honesty and loyalty keep it pure!

I may happen to forget my name,
But never will I forget that I love you for sure

I may not know the future,
But I know my heart,
Which became alive when our love found its start!

Caught by the immensity of your beauty
My sentiments would be justified by your quality!

You are what is going on in the fireplace, that makes others acknowledge
the chimney!
The smiles on my face come from a sea of happiness that you represent
inside of me.

I may not be able to explain how
But you do miracles.
To the might of your sweetness, my heart and I bow!
You comfortably dwell in the cradle of my soul.
Loving like crazy, my heart has accomplished its goal!

You are marvelously marvelous,
The magnetic force that pulls my heart best
Trust that we have acquired over the years
Is the deepest root of our love
We share smiles, and tears
In all obstacles, we've come out above!

I admire you for being such a true woman
I will passionately love you now and then!

We went through our college years together, pushing each other, cheering for each other, supporting each other, and loving each other. We became friends, lovers, study partners, and spiritual advisors. The Lord put us together and protected our love through it all, even when we made some decisions without Him. God's love is so wonderful! His love is everlasting. "For God so loved the world that He gave His only begotten Son, that whoever believes in Him should not perish but have everlasting life" (John 3:16, NKJV). It doesn't matter who you are or what you have done; His love for you has no limit. You have never done too much or gone too far for the Lord! He is always reaching for you and always calling you. He loves you with all His heart. He has great plans for you—plans of peace, plans of happiness, plans of victory, plans of life eternal!

When Heandel and I didn't know what we were going to do with our relationship, the Lord had a plan for us. When we were not sure if we were going to get married because of our differences in our beliefs, the Lord had already paved the way for our future. We just needed to trust Him and know that He was there with us every step of the way. There is one more thing that Heandel and I have in common: we both love the Lord and give Him the first place in our hearts. Although we love each other very much, we both never wanted to put our love before our love for God. Heandel was born and raised as a Baptist, and I became a Seventh-day Adventist after God had shown me where He wanted me to be. The Bible communicates so many times that we should always put God first in everything, and He will take care of it all. Here are some verses concerning that:

"Jesus replied: "'Love the Lord your God with all your heart and with all your soul and with all your mind'"" (Matt. 22:37, NIV).

"But seek first his kingdom and his righteousness, and all these things will be given to you as well" (Matt. 6:33, NIV).

"Love the LORD your God with all your heart and with all your soul and with all your strength" (Deut. 6:5, NIV).

"Do not store up for yourselves treasures on earth, where moths and vermin destroy, and where thieves break in and steal. But store up for yourselves treasures in heaven, where moths and vermin do not destroy, and where thieves do not break in and steal. For where your treasure is, there your heart will be also" (Matt. 6:19–21, NIV).

"But seek His kingdom, and these things will be added to you" (Luke 12:31, NASB 1995).

"Whatever you do in word or deed, *do* all in the name of the Lord Jesus, giving thanks through Him to God the Father" (Colossians 3:17, NASB 1995).

"When all things are subjected to Him, then the Son Himself also will be subjected to the One who subjected all things to Him, so that God may be all in all" (1 Cor. 15:28, NASB 1995).

"He is before all things, and in Him all things hold together" (Col. 1:17, NASB 1995).

"Anyone who loves their father or mother more than me is not worthy of me; anyone who loves their son or daughter more than me is not worthy of me" (Matt. 10:37, NIV).

"Trust in the LORD with all your heart, and do not lean on your own understanding. In all your ways acknowledge Him, and He will make straight your paths" (Prov. 3:5, 6, NASB 1995).

"I am the LORD; that is my name; my glory I give to no other, nor my praise to carved idols" (Isa. 42:8, ESV).

As evidenced all throughout the Bible as well as in our own personal experience, Heandel and I have known without a doubt that if we put God first, He will make a way where there seems to be no way. Although we love each other deeply, we both knew that we couldn't leave our faith just for us to be together in the same church. We prayed, cried, struggled, and experienced some sleepless nights because we didn't know what to do. His mother even called me one day and told me, "*Pitit fi m, mwen renmen w anpil. Vi n jwenn nou non*" meaning, "My daughter, I love you so much. Come to us."

I remember the answer the Lord put in my mouth right away: "I love you, too, Mommy, but I can't do that to God. I did not choose to become a Seventh-day Adventist; the Lord guided me there." I would have made her happy, Heandel happy, and everyone in the family happy, but my major concern was if God would have taken pleasure in that decision. I loved his mother; I loved everyone in his family. I loved the way they made me feel special around them. I always liked the way everyone made me feel when I visited his old church. The members were so nice; they knew how to make people feel welcome. I loved Brother Dorancy, who was always giving us good advice. I loved Sister Malary as well as Brother Malary, a funny man who always had jokes or funny rhyming allegories. They were all wonderful people, and I was so happy that they were in my life. Regardless of everything and everyone, I chose to please the Lord first, and Heandel chose to please the Lord first, and we decided to put an end to our beautiful relationship. It was devastating. I couldn't sleep at night. I cried during the day; I cried at night. I couldn't live with the idea that my love and I were no longer together. No more long hours on the phone. No more beautiful poems. No more "*Je t'aime, mon amour*" before going to sleep. It was hard. It was unbearable, but we had to live with it. We had to put God first.

The Lord was with us every step of the way, even when we didn't understand, even when we didn't even know it. One Sabbath, one old lady at church called me and told me she had a dream about me. In her dream there was a fashion show that included me and another young lady. She said the other woman was wearing jewelry, but I didn't have any jewelry on me. The other young lady came and left the stage. When it was my turn, I walked nicely and beautifully with a smile, and the young man who was in charge of the show picked me and put a seal with the number six on me. He said, "I picked you because your love is pure. You love me for who I am." The dream didn't really mean anything to me at the time, but I understood the dream later, after Heandel proposed to me and told me the size of the ring is six.

Before all that happened though, there was one sleepless Saturday night where I was tossing and turning my head over my pillow, which was wet with tears, but I finally fell asleep and began to dream. In the dream, I was troubled and confused. Sister Marie Jude, the music ministry leader at Gethsemane, who also became a person of honor at our wedding, a wonderful lady, came to comfort me. She was there in the dream telling me that everything was going to be okay. In the morning, I woke up and went to the church for the Pathfinder and Adventurer club meetings. Everyone was asking me if I was okay because I looked like someone who has been sick for weeks. Then Sister Marie Jude came, and I told her the dream. She started to tell me about her experience with her husband. She said she wasn't always an Adventist. She was a fervent Catholic when she met her husband, but after studying the Bible, she became a Seventh-day Adventist and started to keep the Sabbath of the Lord. Right then God put in my head the idea of asking her husband, Elder Joseph, to study the Bible with Heandel. He happily said yes, and they started to study together. Some of the things started to get clearer to Heandel. He was convinced about the seventh day Sabbath of the Lord. He started to join me at Gethsemane every Sabbath. People started to question why he was attending church both on Sabbath with me and on Sunday with his parents. He continued to study the Bible with Dr. Jean Marie Charles, who was the pastor at Gethsemane at that time.

One day, I was asked to do the welcome words for Sabbath. I started to describe how beautiful the Sabbath is and how important it is to God. I used Scripture to explain that we will even observe the Sabbath in heaven, such as: "And it shall come to pass, that from one new moon to another, and from one sabbath to another, shall all flesh come to worship before me, saith the LORD" (Isa. 66:23, KJV). After my presentation, Heandel was impressed about the fact that we will also observe the Sabbath in heaven with the Lord. He said to me, "The Lord really takes the Sabbath seriously."

One beautiful Thursday while I was at work, I gave him a regular call, and he told me to call the pastor to let him know that he was ready to get baptized. I was so excited! I felt like jumping up and down like a little child!

I was filled with joy, and the dream I had in which I saw sister Marie Jude telling me that everything was going to be okay came back to me. I called Pastor Jean Marie Charles right away. He was happy as well. I could hear the joy in his voice. I gave him Heandel's phone number, and he called him right away and arranged the baptism ceremony the same day. He called the head deacon, who was Brother Jean Hyppolite, and baptized Heandel in the name of the Father, the Son, and the Holy Spirit, and welcomed Heandel to the Seventh-day Adventist Church.

On the Sabbath of that week, when Pastor Jean Marie Charles joyfully presented Heandel as a baptized member of the church, there were cries of "HALLELUJAH!" and "Praise the Lord!" mostly from the older ladies, my many Gethsemane mothers. Those ladies were hugging me and praising the Lord with me after the church service. I was overwhelmed with joy! God had done it. He had told me that everything was going to be alright when I was crying that Saturday night. The Lord is awesome! He always keeps His promise. He never leaves us when we are going through the Red Sea of our lives. He never lets us experience the fiery furnace alone. He is always there. We just need to trust Him. I love that hymn, "Trust and Obey," which goes, "Trust and obey, for there's no other way To be happy in Jesus, but to trust and obey" (*The Seventh-day Adventist Hymnal*, hymn 590).

CHAPTER NINE

The Sabbath

God convinced Heandel of the Sabbath, and there was no turning back for him. Through Bible study he discovered that the Sabbath is the memorial of Creation. Our Creator rested on that day to commemorate His Creation. "Then God saw everything that He had made, and indeed *it was* very good" (Gen. 1:31, NKJV). God Himself rested on the Sabbath. "It is a sign between me and the children of Israel for ever: for in six days the LORD made heaven and earth, and on the seventh day he rested, and was refreshed" (Exod. 31:17, KJV). As noticed in this verse, even though the children of Israel are mentioned, it is about the Sabbath of Creation. Let's do a little cause and effect exercise. What is the cause or reason for the action? "…for in six days the LORD made heaven and earth"; What is the effect or the result of the action? "He rested, and was refreshed." Was God tired? Absolutely not! God is never tired. He did it to show us that the day was important to Him. As His children, we need to be obedient and follow His will—not our will, not our traditions, not our heart, not our friends, but His will. Put God first, and everything else will follow. God did not only rest on the Sabbath but He also blessed it and sanctified it.

Thus, the heavens and the earth were finished, and all the host of them. And on the seventh day God ended His work which he had made; and he rested on the seventh day from all his work which He had made. And God blessed the seventh day, and sanctified it: because that in it he had rested from all his work which God created and made. (Gen. 2:1–3, KJV)

How much clearer do we need this to be? It is said that the reason why God sanctified the Sabbath is because He had rested from all His work.

To this day, I am grateful for the blessing of rest and
fellowship on the Sabbath.

When I had just started college, one of my cousins who worked for Bell Atlantic told me she would find me a job there, and I would only need to work one Saturday every month. I thanked her very much for the offer, but I couldn't accept it. She didn't understand my response because she had been sure that I was going to be happy and accept such a job. She said, "You should be happy and take the opportunity because you have been in the US for only a few years, and if you find a job like that, you should be excited." I told her the seventh day of the week is the Sabbath of the Lord, and this is the day that I go to church to praise Him.

She asked, "Why do you have to spend all day in church anyway? Can the pastor feed you when you are hungry?" I took a few seconds before responding, and the Lord quickly put the answer in my mouth. I told her, "You know, dear cousin, I don't go to church for the pastor, and the Sabbath has nothing to do with the pastor. I believe that God will give me a good job that will not require me to work on Sabbath!"

God really did help me find a good job that did not require me to work on Sabbath. Not only that but I also had my summer off, and I got paid every two weeks. One day while I was working as a hostess in a restaurant, a man came in, and I welcomed him and guided him to his seat like I usually do for every customer. While going to his seat, he introduced himself and told me he was Haitian and heard me speak French with an African guy who also worked at the restaurant. He asked me if I like what I do as a job, and I told him that it was an okay job for now. Then, he told me that he was going to help me find a better job and asked me where I go to school. I told him I was attending Medgar Evers College. He said, "Okay, I'm going to come and get you and take you to apply for the job. You will be working for the Board of Education of New York."

While at the Board of Education office, I didn't know much about what to do. The man actually filled out the application for me; all I had to do was sign my name. It was done! A few weeks later, I was called for an interview and got hired as a paraprofessional for the city of New York. When I told my cousin who offered me a job at Bell Atlantic about it, she said, "Wow, you are lucky! I have a friend who was born here and speaks good English who has been trying to find a job like that for a long time. Every time she applied, she never even received a call. I can't believe it," she continued.

I said, "You need to believe it. It's true, and it has nothing to do with luck. It's all God! When I told you that God was going to give me a job that would not require me to work on Sabbath, I was sure He was going to do it. I just didn't know how. I just didn't know it was going to be that good! HALLELUJAH! All praise to the Lord Almighty!!!"

As mentioned in the book, *Seventh-day Adventists Believe*, "The Sabbath commandment functions as the seal of God's law. Generally, seals contain three elements: the name of the owner of the seal, his title, and jurisdiction" (p. 284; see also p. 253 for more information on the Sabbath).

When a person observes the Sabbath, that person openly declares that he or she belongs to the Creator. Jesus Himself pointed to His jurisdiction or legal authority of the Sabbath. In Mark 2:27, 28, He declared, "The sabbath was made for man, and not man for the sabbath: Therefore the Son of man is Lord also of the Sabbath" (KJV). Jesus is showing His divine authority, and He has the power to cancel it if He wanted to, but on the contrary, He did quite the opposite. He declared that it is a blessing for humanity. It was made for humans, for the blessing of everyone who chooses to observe it. Also, talking about the end of time, Jesus declared in Matthew 24:20, "…Pray that your flight may not be in winter or on the Sabbath" (NKJV). The whole chapter of Matthew 24 is talking about the end of time. No one can say this is about the past or that He was talking about the Israelites.

The disciples also observed the Sabbath. After Jesus' death, they prepared His body and then went home to observe the Sabbath. "And they returned, and prepared spices and ointments; and rested the sabbath day according to the commandment" (Luke 23:56, KJV). The commandment that was mentioned in this passage was the fourth commandment. Do we still think that it is important, or do we want to follow humanity's traditions? The Sabbath is a time of fellowship. It is a time to relax and forget about our everyday troubles as well as to spend quality time with the Creator, family, and friends in a spiritual mindset. *"C'est un jour de fête!"* (It is a day of celebration!) We will celebrate the Sabbath in heaven with our Lord and Savior, our Creator and Redeemer, and with all the righteous from around the world!

CHAPTER TEN

The Next Few Years

Engagement

One beautiful spring day, Heandel told me to get straight home after work because he was taking me out. Since we didn't often go out, especially on a weekday, I had the idea that something special was about to happen. We used to mostly spend time studying or going for a walk or having long conversations on the phone. I went and got a nice French manicure. When I got home, a handsome, brown-eyed young man was waiting for me. When I saw him with his beautiful brown suit, I was sure he was going to ask the question that I had been wanting to answer. We had already known each other and been in love for over five years. We had just graduated college. I was ready to spend the rest of my life with the love of my life. Since he was wearing a brown suit, I decided to wear a nice brown dress-suit that matched his. He had already planned for a black taxi to pick us up at my house. Then we headed to Manhattan.

I felt so special and loved that day. He was holding my hand and telling me, "*Je t'aime, mon amour*" (I love you, my love) throughout the drive. His eyes were contemplating mine. He gently kissed me and told me, "*Tu es si belle*" (You are so beautiful). When we got to our destination, I was amazed to see that he was taking me to one of the most prestigious restaurants in Manhattan. It was one of Bill Clinton's favorites when he was in New York. To get in the restaurant, a man must wear a tie. The name of the restaurant is 21. It is situated on 50th Street and 21st Street in Manhattan. The food was delicious, and the decor was exquisite, but my attention was mostly on my love. I was checking his every move and enjoying the smell of his cologne. He decided to read a beautiful poem he wrote for me just for the occasion. After reading the poem, he went down on his knees, handed me a beautiful rose, and asked me to open it. When I opened it, I saw a beautiful ring that perfectly matched my personality. It was exquisitely beautiful but not overly extravagant. We both were emotional. I said, "Yes!" with tears of joy. He planned everything so well. There was a vase of beautiful red roses that he ordered. Everything was perfect. I didn't want the night to end. I was treated like a true princess. I felt like the happiest woman in the world because I was going to marry the love of my life.

I don't know how he was able to get a ring that fit me just right without taking me to try it on. When I asked him, he answered, "Just by holding your hands, I was able to measure the size of your ring finger." When he told me the size was six, it reminded me of the dream the older lady at my church had for me. (Remember: The young man who was in charge of the fashion show picked me up and put a seal with the number six on me. He said, "I picked you because your love is pure. You love me for who I am.") When she told me the dream, it made no sense, but knowing the size of the ring made the dream become a reality.

Heandel and I were so happy together.

Wedding Day

Our wedding was beautiful. I will never forget that beautiful autumn day. Everything was arranged with great detail and thought. The decor was made by my friend, Yvrose Desormes, who is an event decorator. She did her job with love and exquisitely arranged the colors for my wedding. She used beautiful gold, the color of wealth, and white, the color of purity. Natural bouquets of white flowers mixing with some yellow ones were all over, from the entrance to the church altar. The flower girls, bridesmaids, Bible carrier, princes and princesses included more than twenty people. My brother, Wilner, was so handsome and proud of his African prince title as he held the hand of a beautiful young lady dressed as an African princess.

Everything was on point. The parents happily entered and followed the procession. When it was my time to enter with my beautiful white wedding dress and white veil, my heart was beating so hard. Tears started to drop from my eyes when my love, my charming prince, surprised me with a beautiful and romantic poem that he wrote for the occasion. The poem is title "*Ma Belle et Moi Allons Nous Marier*" which means, "My Beautiful and I Are Getting Married." The same way Solomon did not hide his feelings for his beloved one, my precious love did not hesitate to express his feelings for me. That day, he publicly described his love for me. His words were so profound. The expression of his voice was so emotional. I could feel his heart, even though I was at the entrance waiting for him to finish this beautiful poem. In my heart I was saying, *I am so in love with this man. I am so blessed to get married to the love of my life today.*

When my father came to give me away, I could tell that he was happy. Before taking my hand from my father, Heandel gave him a military salute. That day I saw joy mingled with pride in my father's face. Our friend, poet Jean Elie Barjon, did a beautiful, poetic presentation, and right after him, the master of ceremonies, Dr. Johnson Cesar, couldn't contain his joy. He said, "It will be difficult to talk after that man." I said in my heart, *This man is a great speaker himself, but still he is complimenting another speaker with great eloquence.* One could say that it takes a great one to know a great one. My beautiful sister in Christ, Dr. Fabienne Gaillard Ulysse, did the Scripture reading with elegance and beauty. Our pastor was so happy to be the one celebrating our wedding, not only because he was the one who baptized Heandel but also because he loved both of us, in general. We loved him as well. He was and still is a wonderful man of God.

I felt really blessed when Pastor Ner Jean Pierre was doing the intercessory prayer. He fervently asked the Lord to open the windows of heaven and pour down His blessing upon me and Heandel. My wedding was beautiful, poetic, romantic, eloquent, and spiritual. Sister Marie Jude Joseph, one of the people that God showed me in a dream that was comforting me when I needed help, was one of the people of honor. She sang "The Lord's Prayer" beautifully. Sister Carole Saint Ange, another person of honor, read a poem written for the occasion. Everything was exactly the way I wanted it to be. Beautiful, elegant, romantic, poetic, and spiritual. The pianist, Andy Voltaire, played wonderful, traditional wedding pieces. Yves Deshomme also played one of my favorite violin pieces. After the church ceremony, a reception followed.

The ambiance at the reception hall was inviting. The bridal party made their entrance fun and joyful. Everyone was happy to see two adorable kids dressed as the little bride and groom as well as the beautiful flower girls. Then the bridesmaids and the young groomsmen each made a special entrance act. As souvenirs, we gave each person a CD made especially for the occasion. On the cover of the CD, there were these words: "Suzette and Heandel; Two Poets, Two Lovers: One Great Match Made in Heaven." We are definitely one great match made by God. If it wasn't for the Lord, we would not have been together. God has shown us His presence in our marriage in many ways.

Marital Life

Marrying Heandel, the man I love, has been one of the greatest blessings that I have received from God. Many more blessings and miracles came during our marital life's journey. A few months before our wedding, we moved to Georgia and began looking for jobs while we were living at a friend's house. By the grace of God, we both were able to find jobs. We were able to have money to rent a beautiful apartment to move into after our wedding. The first night we slept in our apartment was memorable. Coming from over a twelve-hour drive from New York to Georgia, we were exhausted, but we were happy to be married and living together in our apartment. We prayed, thanking God for protecting us on the road, and we asked Him to bless our apartment. We showered and ate dinner on a table made from a box and covered with a nice tablecloth. We sat on the floor and ate our dinner, looking at each other and saying how happy we were to be in our own home as husband and wife. We made our bed on a carpeted floor and slept holding each other.

The next day we had to go to work. Right after work, we went hand in hand to Rooms-to-Go, a furniture store not far from where we lived. We bought our first bedroom set, which was simple, nice, and comfortable. We slept on our first bed with the same attitude that we slept on the floor the night before, so happy to be together, so happy to have each other. We didn't have much, but we were happy. Love is what we had then, and it is still keeping us happy to this day. We started with nothing but love. We both were pre-k lead teachers. We put together our paychecks to buy every piece of furniture we needed for our two-bedroom apartment. One month later, we were so happy to learn that we were going to have a baby. During the whole period of pregnancy, we both were able to work to pay our bills and save a little. There was no morning sickness. We both were able to work and continue to earn our salaries. We had in total five different baby showers. The parents, the other teachers, friends from church, and friends from *Sonje Ayiti* (Remember Haiti), a non-profit organization of which I used to be a member, all brought gifts for the baby. Even the crib we had was a gift. Our baby bottles were not even purchased with our own money.

We only had to plan for our precious little princess to arrive. Although we had our jobs, our apartment, and our new church in Georgia, I wanted to go back to New York for the baby's delivery since she was due in June. I wanted to be with family members. After the end of the school year, we both were on vacation. We drove our van to New York. Heandel drove all the way, and I mostly slept and ate and got out when we took little breaks.

First Baby Girl

I am not sure if having our daughter in New York was a wise decision. The Lord knows why He let certain things happen. Everything was going great until the day I had my baby. The night before the due date, I went to the hospital and told them that I saw liquid coming out of me. The nurse that was checking me said not to worry if I didn't feel any contractions. She told me I should just go home and come back when I feel any pain. I followed her advice and went back home to my parent's house. Early in the morning, I started to feel pain, and my beautiful mother-in-law and my father-in-law took me to the hospital. The pain was not unbearable. It kept on coming and going. However, I was on monitors. The doctor said that I needed an epidural to help me induce because I wasn't dilated. Oh my, I don't know if the person who gave me the epidural was doing it for the first time or what, but he had to do it more than once. That was the worst pain I ever felt my entire life. I felt like I was about to die from that needle. I wish I knew better and stayed in Georgia to have my baby. I probably wouldn't have experienced as much trauma as I did.

After the epidural I stayed on my bed waiting for what was coming next. It was my first time having a baby. I didn't know any better. While waiting, I heard a weird voice in the machine that was monitoring my precious little one. Then I saw many doctors and nurses running towards me, and they rushed me to another room. All I heard was the voice of a doctor saying, "The baby's heartbeat is dropping! We have to take her for an emergency C-section!"

The last thing I saw was a light that was getting dimmer, and I said, "*Jésus, san w te koule pou mwen tou wi!*" ("Jesus, your blood was shed for me as well!")

When I was able to return to myself, I felt so cold like I was in a freezer. All the blankets they put on me weren't enough. I had a fever, and my right hand was numb. However, I was so happy to hear that my baby was alive. She was taken to the intensive care unit. A nice and beautiful Haitian nurse came to me and said, "Today, I witnessed a miracle. If we had waited one more minute, your baby would have not survived because the umbilical cord was looped around her neck." She continued and said, "Some mucus had already gone into her lungs. That's why we are keeping her in the intensive care unit for a week."

When I was able to see my precious little one for the first time, tears of joy and mixed feelings came from my eyes. Although in the intensive care unit, she looked strong and ready to start her journey. She looked determined to embark on the train of life. Born weighing eight pounds and with a firm body, my precious little one was ready to start following the steps that Jesus made possible for her. I was so happy holding my baby. I didn't want to let go when the nurse told me the visitation time was over, and I had to leave. Leaving the hospital without my baby was so hard for me, even when I knew it was only for three more days. I cried harder than when I was in labor. However, I was grateful that the Lord blessed me and my baby and kept us alive.

At the end of the summer, we drove back to Georgia in order to get back to work. My beautiful sister-in-law, Mideline, drove back with us and was so happy to help us set the crib and the decor for our precious little one. She was the joy of our life and our miracle baby. Her physical and spiritual development over the years prove to me every day that my God is able and with Him anything is possible.

Because of her traumatic birth, my baby girl was diagnosed with a development and speech delay. Doctors weren't sure if she would be able to walk. However, on a beautiful Sabbath in January 2007, while we were celebrating the wedding anniversary of a beautiful couple, my baby girl started to walk!!! Somebody was handing a cellphone to her and asked her to come and get it. Everyone was so happy and said, "HALLELUJAH!" to praise God for that beautiful testimony. Not only was she able to walk but she can now, by the grace of God, run, ride a bicycle, and do most of the things kids her age are able to do. She loves to read and is doing great academically. She loves church activities. One Sabbath, while she was still a toddler, the person who was doing the children's story didn't pick her to pray even when her hand was up. She cried so loud that the whole church was able to hear her. The elder in service that day said, "Please, don't ever skip her again. She likes to pray, so let her pray."

Second Baby Girl

Three years after the birth of my first baby girl, my God blessed me with a second baby girl. With two beautiful princesses to admire, I was so happy to be a mother. Her birth was a planned C-section, and everything went well. Even the epidural didn't hurt as much as the one I had to endure in New York. We had everything we needed for my cute little one, and I was so happy to take my princess with me when I was leaving the hospital.

A few months after her birth, we heard about her having a hole in her heart. We gave that matter to the Lord, and He took care of it. I don't even know how it happened, but my God Almighty did it. The doctors revealed that the hole was gone. HALLELUJAH! My princess' heart was healed! My Jesus did it again! Another miracle in my life. She grew up well, and she now has a flexible body that helps her to do her gymnastics moves. She loves to draw and make clothes for her dolls. She likes to read and write. She likes helping others and telling others about Jesus. I am so thankful for both of my daughters!

CHAPTER ELEVEN

My Friend Nolcy

If living in Georgia brought me some difficult experiences, it also brought some wonderful ones. One of the best experiences I had from my years in Georgia was the blessing of meeting Nolcy, my friend, sister, and prayer partner. She is a wonderful and phenomenal lady. She was in the labor and delivery room with me when I was giving birth to my second princess. She was there, praying and singing hymns with me, while the doctors and nurses were doing their jobs. It was a safe and almost painless delivery. I praise God for putting Nolcy on my path. She continues to be a source of encouragement in my life. She is more than a sister to me. We always bring each other's burdens to the throne of grace. Through the years, we have learned to cry together in prayer, praise God together, and share testimonies. God put Nolcy in my life to help me grow spiritually, to help me have a better relationship with Him.

No Sugarcoating with Nolcy

My dear and beautiful friend Nolcy always tells it as it is. She is not fake. You have to either love her and know that you can count on her because her yes is yes and her no is no, or hate her if you don't like to hear the truth. She never sugarcoats the truth for me. If I am wrong, she will always tell me that I am wrong. One day, something happened at our church. An older sister was not being nice to me, and I burst out a general statement about the ladies in the church. Right then, in front of everyone, Nolcy told me that the statement was wrong. She said, "You need to state your problem with the person with whom you have a problem. Do not generalize all the ladies because one lady was unkind to you." I was not happy at that moment, but I needed to hear that truth at that specific time because my statement simply wasn't true and didn't reflect well on me or the women of the church. Nolcy said, "What if a visitor hears you speak like that?" Although there were no visitors around, I had to accept that what she said was true and keep calm.

Another day, I had an issue with my husband, and I was really mad about something that he had said to me. I called Nolcy expecting her to be on my side, but she said to me, "You are wrong, sis. You need to go apologize to your husband." Once again, she didn't tell me what I felt like hearing, but she told it to me as it was. Even though I was very angry at my husband, I had to breathe, pray, and go apologize. It was the right thing to do, and my relationship with him was better for it.

She's a Prayer Warrior

Nolcy is a prayer warrior. She is someone who taught me about praying without ceasing. She prays all the time. When she is happy, when she is sad, when everything is well, and when there are troubles, she is always praying. Through her, I have learned to use some of David's psalms as mine. I have learned to memorize many of them and use them as my spiritual weapons. She would put her activities aside to spend hours praying and fasting with me. She taught me some old hymns that are not being sung in church anymore. I call them her "dad's songs" because her dad was an old pastor who knew all these old hymns that most people in church don't sing anymore. Those old hymns are powerful; their meaningful words inspire faith and strength.

My friend and prayer partner, Nolcy (on the left), poses with me.

The Morning Worship Hymns

I didn't grow up in a devoted Christian household; therefore, I wasn't used to having morning worship. I didn't know any morning songs. I didn't even know that the hymnal has one specific section for morning worship until I started to pray with Nolcy every morning. One of these hymns from the French hymnal is titled, "*Pour moi l'aurore*" (The Dawn For Me) (*Hymnes et Louanges*, hymn 414), and another one is called, "*Que ta lumière*" (May Your Light) (*Hymnes et Louanges*, hymn 411). These hymns are sung with the purpose of inviting God in your heart to start your day. These are morning devotional hymns. Morning devotion should be the first thing a Christian does before starting with the craziness of this life. Psalm 5:3 states, "My voice shalt thou hear in the morning, O LORD; in the morning will I direct my prayer unto thee, and will look up" (KJV).

Inherited Prayer

There are so many prayers that I inherited from Nolcy's dad, Pastor Fenelon Destin. Through Nolcy, I learned many powerful words of prayers. One of the best ones that I mostly use is: "Oh Lord, see for me what I cannot see! Hear for me what I cannot hear! Go for me where I cannot go! Destroy all my enemies' wicked plans against me, and give me victory always in the name of Jesus!" These words of prayer have become mine, and I want to thank my friend, my spiritual sister for them, who inherited them from her father and shared them with me. They are more precious than gold.

Precious Treasures

I have been so blessed to inherit those precious treasures from Pastor Fenelon Destin, a man who I only physically met three short times in my life. Through Nolcy, I have learned how wonderful this man

What I like about these treasures is that they can't be sold out or bought. They are free, but you can only earn them by being patient and practical. They only make sense when you learn how to use them personally. They only make sense when they become part of your life. They only make sense when they become your daily bread.

was. I have realized that Nolcy got her prayer inheritance from him. She then passed on these precious things to me. I am so rich because of these precious treasures that I can use all the time. Pastor Destin is sleeping with the other saints now and waiting for our Jesus to come back. However, his precious treasures have been passed on to others. His precious treasures have been passed on to me, and I am teaching them to my children. I believe that these treasures will be passed on from generation to generation until our Lord and Savior Jesus Christ comes to take us with Him. What I like about these treasures is that they can't be sold out or bought. They are free, but you can only earn them by being patient and practical. They only make sense when you learn how to use them personally. They only make sense when they become part of your life. They only make sense when they become your daily bread. In Philippians 4:6, 7, the Bible says, "Do not be anxious about anything, but in every situation, by prayer and petition, with thanksgiving, present your requests to God. And the peace of God, which transcends all understanding, will guard your hearts and your minds in Christ Jesus" (NIV).

In 2021, I wrote a poem in French that includes an acrostic for Nolcy's father. I'm including it here as a tribute to this man of God.

Cap-Haïtien,
Fière Cité des Haïtiens,
D'où se dresse Vertières,
Cité du Cap-Haïtien
Vieille cité d'hommes fièrs
Et de femmes à la tête altière!

Cap-Haïtien,
Fière Cité des Haïtiens,
Ah! sur cette éminence,
Avec foi et vaillance,
Haïti a tracé son destin,
Pointant au monde de la liberté le chemin.

Cap-Haïtien,
Fière Cité des Haïtiens,
C'est aussi le berceau de Fénelon Destin,
Qu'un février, comme d'un divin dessein,
D'un air doux, tranquille et sage,
Dieu fit épanouir dans notre entourage

Pour nous montrer du Ciel le chemin.
Pour cet homme d'immense destin,
C'était le seul mandat, l'unique gage!

Fidèle propagateur de l'Évangile.
Excellent, humble et gentil,
Naturelement attentif
Et surtout diligent envers tout esprit captif,
Luttait-il contre l'esclavage du péché
Optait-il toujours pour la divine liberté,
Noyau dur de la chrétienté et sûr de l'éternité!

Dévoué corps et âme à son Sauveur
Enseignait-il à tous de tout son cœur
Son évangile, celui de Dieu, sans peur!
Toujours et sans cesse il louait son Créateur!
Impayable fut-il ce valeureux serviteur
Noble de cœur et si fidèle à son Seigneur!

The poem speaks of Cap-Haïtien, the city where he was born, and pays tribute to Pastor Destin's kind and humble spirit as a faithful propagator of the gospel, fighting against the slavery of sin.

Spiritual Connection

Nolcy and I have a spiritual connection that I am not sure I know how to describe. Sometimes certain things may be happening in my spiritual life, and God reveals it to her. Certain things might be happening in her life, and God reveals it to me as well. One day, out of nowhere, I started to explain to her what happened to a friend of mine in Haiti. She was so shocked not because of what happened to my friend, but because God revealed to her something to do about it. It had been something she was already praying about in her heart. You know those types of prayers that you can only pray in your heart because they are so intimate? This is the type of prayer that God answered for her that morning while I was just in her kitchen eating breakfast after walking with her at a

What we, as children of God, need to know is to listen and follow God's will because He knows what's best.

neighborhood park. Sometimes God reveals something to us and wants us to share it. Other times, He wants us to wait. That beautiful morning God wanted me to tell my friend that testimony right away because He knew that she needed it right away. What we, as children of God, need to know is to listen and follow God's will because He knows what's best.

God's will

Another prayer that I have learned from my friend Nolcy is, "God, help me to follow your will even when I don't like or understand it!" It took me time to adjust and start to use this prayer as my own because I wasn't sure that I really wanted to do that. However, I have learned that this is one of the best prayers to say because God's will is best for us. He knows what we don't know. He understands what we don't understand. Jeremiah 29:11 says, "'For I know the plans I have for you,' declares the LORD, 'plans to prosper you and not to harm you, plans to give you hope and a future'" (NIV). God plans for us to have a future. He does not want us to live a miserable life and die. He wants us to choose salvation and inherit eternal life.

Tall, Proud, Black Woman

Nolcy is a tall, proud, black woman, but she is also humble. She is not ashamed to humbly say, "I am sorry," even to a little child when she is wrong. Her strength is not from her height or her physical aptitude. She has that inner strength that makes her exceptional. She has a singular beauty. I describe her as the type of woman the Bible described as virtuous: "Charm is deceitful, and beauty is vain, but a woman who fears the LORD is to be praised" (Prov. 31:30, ESV). Nolcy is the kind of woman who fears the Lord. She has a close relationship with Him. She is not afraid of Him. What she has for Him is reverence and love.

Miles Away but Not Separate

The circumstances of life eventually moved me from Georgia to Virginia, but my connection with Nolcy has grown even stronger. Through technology, we are able to pray together every morning. We can also call each other any time of the day and night when we have some urgent prayer requests. We call them emergency prayers because they can't wait. They have to be done right away. We have experienced so many of those, and we have seen God's omnipotent hands working in our lives many times.

CHAPTER TWELVE

Virginia

In the summer of 2010, while my husband and I and our two beautiful daughters were in New York to spend time with family members, something terrible happened. I lost my loving father. This situation made us stay longer in New York. We mourned together with family members, and I remember that my mother-in-law said she would like to die like that, without spending time in pain and giving people the trouble of taking care of her. Little did we know, what she wanted played out even quicker and faster than my father's death. On a regular day in October 2010 while she was at work, someone found her just sleeping on the floor. She was gone.

Concerning death, we know when the trumpets sound that the dead in Christ will come to life, but we don't know when that will be. We who are still awake need to make sure that we prepare ourselves every day because we don't know the day or hour that our Savior and Lord will appear in the clouds. The Bible says that Jesus will not touch the ground when He comes back. He will not come back as a lamb or a little baby in a manger. He will come in glory. His second coming will be spectacular. "Behold, he cometh with clouds; and every eye shall see him, and they also which pierced him: and all kindreds of the earth shall wail because of him. Even so, Amen" (Rev. 1:7, KJV). "Wherefore if they shall say unto you, Behold, he is in the desert; go not forth: behold, he is in the secret chambers; believe it not. For as the lightning cometh out of the east, and shineth even unto the west; so shall also the coming of the Son of man be" (Matt. 24:26, 27, KJV).

After the death of my mother-in-law, my husband and I stayed in New York longer than we planned because we were both without jobs at that point in time and unsure of what we were going to do next. We went to Connecticut for a little bit and filled out some applications. We didn't find anything and went back to New York. In New York, Sister Yolene Aristomène, a loving woman, referred me to a position as a pre-k lead teacher. While I was waiting to be called for the job, my brother, Wilner, who had just bought a house in Virginia, invited us to come and live in his house. He was about to go on a nine-month deployment for the Navy. He was so happy to have us stay in the house while he was going to be away.

Heandel went to Georgia to bring our belongings to Virginia, and Wilner was about to leave at the same time. Before leaving, my loving brother took me to Sam's Club to buy food because he wanted to make sure there was food in the house for us. I remembered that he picked up the biggest bag of rice that was at Sam's Club. He made sure that we had beans, oil, and other necessary items needed. Then he left for his deployment in early 2011. While he was gone and my husband was in Georgia, the job that I applied for in New York called me for an interview. I was perplexed not knowing exactly what to do: stay in Virginia without a job or go back to New York for a job that was waiting for me? My husband was waiting for me to let him know if he should bring our belongings to Virginia or go to New York with them. I prayed about it and asked a few people what they thought, and I eventually decided to stay in Virginia.

While Heandel was driving to Virginia, the truck stopped working in the middle of the road. He called the truck company, and they referred him to their nearest car repair place. They spent hours trying to fix the truck and realized that the problem was deeper than they thought. They paid for Heandel to spend the night in a hotel. We were so grateful that God provided that time for him to rest. Heandel affirmed he was really tired, but he was also anxious to get back to me and the children. He was able to relax and refresh himself and wake up the next day with more energy. The truck company sent another truck and two men to move our belongings from the broken truck to the other one. An evident problem became a sure blessing. To show us that it was our Lord and Provider who was acting for us, God made it possible for the truck rental company to come to an agreement to return half of our payment. This money was the exact amount that we needed to make our car payment for that month. We were so grateful because we didn't know where we would find the money to make the payment for that month, but God always provides everything for us and our children.

Our First Sabbath in Virginia

Our first Sabbath in Virginia was quite remarkable! It was the second Sabbath of January 2011. My husband and I were on a new adventure with our two beautiful princesses. The oldest one was four, and the youngest one was one year old. It was a new adventure to attend an English-speaking Adventist church. We drove less than ten minutes and went past the church! We were so thankful to have the GPS, which told us to turn around because we had passed our destination. The church building looked simple and plain. The sign that said "Chesapeake Seventh-day Adventist Church" was so small and written on a stone. One could easily just pass by and not be able to see it and drive further just the same way my husband and I had done.

Entering the church, I became aware that our adventure would be even better than I had originally thought. The church was filled with white people! I had never worshipped in a church with people who spoke differently and looked differently than I did. I looked at my husband and came back to reality when a short lady welcomed us with a beautiful smile. She instantly made us feel more at ease. She said, "Welcome to the Chesapeake Seventh-day Adventist Church." She invited us in with a smile and told us about the mother's room if the kids needed a little break. Our youngest one was still in a baby car seat at the time. We thanked her, but we didn't need to use it because our little ones were perfectly quiet at church. I really loved my children's baby stage. They were both quiet babies. They hardly cried and were often content with very little attention. I still don't understand how they grew up to be so loud sometimes.

My husband and I in Virginia.

After the service, that enthusiastic short lady with blonde hair and a tiny body invited us to stay for fellowship lunch. There were many multicultural types of food and desserts. We were also introduced to brothers and sisters from Russia, Romania, Uruguay, El Salvador, Puerto Rico, Guatemala,

Trinidad, France, Haiti, Jamaica, Saint Lucia, Trinidad, and a few other countries that I forget.

The church that I perceived to be a white church happened to be a multicultural church. That melting pot that I lived with in Brooklyn, New York, found its residency in one church building. Everyone seemed happy and comfortable together. That short white lady was everywhere, talking to everyone. She didn't sit at one table to eat her food. She was moving from one table to the next with her food, and her husband didn't sit down at all. He was like a child with a happy case of ADHD. He stayed in the kitchen offering a spicy dip to everyone. He only knew one Spanish phrase and one French phrase that he kept on repeating to everyone he thought spoke another language other than English. He would repeat "*Feliz Navidad*" (Merry Christmas) and "*Bon Secours*" (good help) over and over. Someone said he will say, "*Feliz Navidad*," every Sabbath even when it's not Christmas. When I asked about "*Bon Secours*," he said it was the name of a hospital, but that was the only French he knew, and he would use it regardless.

> *The good news of salvation should not be only taught through words. It needs to be shown through actions.*

These two, the short lady and her funny husband, were one of the best couples I have ever met. Their house was open to everyone. There was often a bonfire or a social activity going on there. My children always enjoyed going there for fun. The husband was called "uncle," and she was everyone's "auntie." My children grew up calling them uncle and auntie. These two have been a great blessing for the church and my family. They have since moved away to another state, and I miss having them around and fellowshipping with them.

The husband was always available to help people fix their cars, cut down trees, and fix other appliances. He seemed to enjoy that just like a kid would enjoy his new toy. They also enjoyed helping people move. I remember when I was moving from my brother's house to mine, this couple and some other church members came to help. At that point, I was eight months and four weeks pregnant with my son. The only thing I was able to do was to cook for everyone. It was great feeding them while they seemed to have so much fun moving my furniture from my brother's house to my own house. These people, mostly men, just enjoy spending their Sundays helping others. They see it as a ministry. Indeed, that is what it is: a ministry because the good news of salvation should not be only taught through words. It needs to be shown through actions. "For it is by grace you have been saved, through faith—and this is not from yourselves, it is the gift of God—not by works, so that no one can boast. For we are God's handiwork, created in Christ Jesus to do good works, which God prepared in advance for us to do" (Eph. 2:8–10, NIV).

God prepared us in advance to do His good work. We can't just sit in church and expect people to do things for us while we are doing nothing. Everyone has something that he or she can do. I don't know how to fix cars, but I can cook for someone who is hungry and who cannot cook for themselves. I can pray for someone who needs prayers. Whatever you can do, do it! Don't wait for someone else to do it.

A Child's Answered Prayers

I remember when my oldest daughter started to pray for a brother. Her best friend started to pray for a brother as well. Both her and her best friend only had a sister, and they wanted a brother. My daughter was five at that time, and her friend was six. God answered both of their prayers at the same time. Her best friend's mother, Marilyn, and I got pregnant at around the same time. Then somehow, the children decided to announce it to the church while they were praying during the children's corner part of the service. Everyone at church was excited after the service, and they started to hug both me and Marilyn with cheers and congratulations. I wasn't ready to give the announcement yet. I was waiting until after I had seen a doctor to confirm, but the news got out before then. It was so sweet when everyone started to give me special attention, asking to touch my belly, and letting me go first in line to get food as well as asking me what I would like to eat.

The church had a double baby shower for me and Marilyn, and it was beautiful. Everything was blue. The decorations, the gift bags, everyone's clothes. That was a beautiful surprise. The gifts were great! I didn't have to worry about buying anything for the baby after the shower. Even diapers and wipes were in great quantity. We had so much fun with the games. The boys remain friends until now. God does answer the prayers of little ones.

My son's middle name is Joshua—named after the biblical character who led the Israelites to Jericho. My son was named after him so, as a family, we may remember God took us to our own place. We bought our house a few weeks before he was born. Every day after work, my husband would go and get the house ready. He found a few friends who helped him paint and do other things that needed to be done before we moved

My life is full of testimony. God has done great things for me. This book is just part of my journey with the Lord.

in. We were so blessed for the friends who helped. Our friend, Johnny, was at the house many times helping my husband. His friend and coworker, Rosalind, also helped tremendously. One Sunday, we had a work bee. People actually came and helped with cleaning and setting things up for the entrance to the house. Wow! We have a wonderful church family. That's the true meaning of agape love.

God has blessed us with wonderful friends wherever we go. My children have been blessed to grow up with loving people. From Vacation Bible School to Sabbath School, my children have received good instructions for their spiritual life.

My life is full of testimonies. God has done great things for me. This book is just part of my journey with the Lord. May these testimonies bring more souls to God's kingdom!

I would like to end with this poem of mine entitled, "Praise:"

Praise

I am here to praise Thee, oh God Almighty!
You have called me even though I am not worthy.
You have called me Your daughter
And have loved me forever!

My life without You had no sense,
Now you give me the essence of existence!

If I could climb countless mountains to shout HALLELUJAH,
This would not have been enough to praise who You are!
You are the Omnipotent, the Omnipresent, the Omniscient!
There is none like You!

You are the One, the only One,
Who can turn a no one into someone.
Who can take a motherless child
Out of darkness and make of her a princess!

You are the One who can turn a nobody into somebody!
You deserve, Lord, all the glory!

Lord, I am standing here today
Because You're in my life everyday
Under Your wings I want to stay.
You are Yahweh
You are the way!

You are the Alpha and the Omega
For you I shout HALLELUJAH!
The One who protects us from Corona
The great Healer, Jehovah-Rapha
You are always there, Jehovah-shammah.
Touch us, oh great Adonai!!!

You were there with me on that Thursday morning
When my heart was deeply hurting.
My husband rushed with me to the hospital
The X-rays didn't give any signal
Stress test revealed nothing
But was it physical
Mental, psychological, or spiritual?

On Friday night in a dream
You, oh Lord, you told me it was a scheme,
The enemy used the extreme
And came up with a mortal theme.
What he seemed to forget is, Yours is the winning team!
You are Elohim!!
You are the same in the morning and evening
For you, I will sing hymns of thanksgiving!

That Friday night, you used my husband
To touch me with your healing hands,
And on Sabbath morning, I was at church with no pain
To praise your name again and again!!!

HALLELUJAH! I praise Thee, oh God Almighty!
My Provider, my Redeemer
My great Healer, my Comforter
I praise Thee, oh Lord my Father!

Our happy family of five.

Bibliography

Hymnes et Louanges. Dammarie-Les-Lys, Paris, France: Les Signes Des Temps, 1951.

Jenson, Kristen A. *Good Pictures Bad Pictures: Porn-Proofing Today's Young Kids.* Kennewick, WA: Glen Cove Press, 2018.

The Seventh-day Adventist Hymnal. Washington, D.C.: Review and Herald Publishing Association, 1985.

Seventh-day Adventists Believe. Boise, ID: Pacific Press Publishing Association, 2005.

TEACH Services, Inc.
P U B L I S H I N G

We invite you to view the complete
selection of titles we publish at:
www.TEACHServices.com

We encourage you to write us
with your thoughts about this,
or any other book we publish at:
info@TEACHServices.com

TEACH Services' titles may be purchased in
bulk quantities for educational, fund-raising,
business, or promotional use.
bulksales@TEACHServices.com

Finally, if you are interested in seeing
your own book in print, please contact us at:
publishing@TEACHServices.com
We are happy to review your manuscript at no charge.